TECHNOLOGY AND RELIGION

IS VOLUME

94

OF THE

Twentieth Century Encyclopedia of Catholicism

UNDER SECTION

IX

THE CHURCH AND THE MODERN WORLD

IT IS ALSO THE

115TH

VOLUME IN ORDER OF PUBLICATION

Edited by HENRI DANIEL-ROPS *of the Académie Française*

TECHNOLOGY AND RELIGION

By *HENRI QUEFFÉLEC*

Translated from the French by S. J. TESTER

HAWTHORN BOOKS · PUBLISHERS · *New York*

First Edition, February, 1964

NIHIL OBSTAT

Joannes M. T. Barton, S.T.D., L.S.S.

   Censor Deputatus

IMPRIMATUR

✠ Georgius L. Craven

   Episcopus Sebastopolis, Vicarius Generalis

Westmonasterii, die XXVIII NOVEMBRIS MCMLXIII

BL 240.2
Q 3 t

H-9553

CONTENTS

INTRODUCTION

The reader of the title of this little book, whether he is a
Christian or not, may well exclaim: "What! Another one?"
And his reaction would be reasonable as so many books and
pamphlets have been written by Christians of all denomina-
tions on the same, or a similar, subject: H. U. von Balthasar,
Maritain, Sherwood Taylor, Fr Victor White, and, in this
series, Jean Abelé and Paul Chauchard; and, among non-
Catholic writers, Canon Raven, C. A. Coulson and E. L.
Mascall, to name but a few.

But a Christian writer should be too deeply concerned for
the spiritual cooperation of all men and too anxious to take
part in a collective and profitable task either to wish to be
original or to worry for a moment because the statement of
his theme calls to mind others' treatment of the same ideas.
There are bound to be similarities; but not only is it impossible to avoid them—one should not try to. Should an
orchestra refuse to play Mozart's A major concerto,
because some other orchestra has played it in the same year?
Should a soloist feel obliged to play a passage wrongly
because a predecessor has played it carefully and correctly?
But comparisons are never reasons: a piece of eighteenth-
century music does not change, whereas the world, the real
world before our eyes, is always moving and changing and,
especially, what is called technological progress has in the
last twenty or thirty years outstripped all forecasts and
expectations. For Christians of the twentieth century, who
can do many things but cannot divorce themselves from their
own age, the clash between their beliefs and ways of life

which are continuously changing can only constitute a terrible, an agonizing problem. And it is only to be expected that Christians, because of the way they look at things, should try very seriously to define that problem and to examine it before outlining a solution.

On December 25th, 1961, Pope John XXIII published the Bull *Humanae salutis*, convening the Second Vatican Council. We have all heard and read a good deal about the Council, and we all say, with reference to this or that article, that it will have a great importance in the history of the Church. But we do not really believe what we say and generally tend to minimize the rôle of the Council by regarding as its specific task the bringing together of the different Christian denominations. But this problem, though no one can deny its urgency or its vastness, can only properly be seen in the context of a still vaster project, the confrontation of the eternal Church with all the facts of the modern world. In a style, the calm solemnity of which is married with great power, *Humanae salutis* explicitly emphasized this purpose:

> At a time when mankind is at a turning-point, entering a new age, the Church is faced with tasks of immense gravity and vastness, as she was in the most tragic times in her history. We have to bring into contact with the life-giving and perpetual forces of the Gospel this modern world, a world glorying in its progress in the fields of technology and science, but suffering consequences in the temporal order, which some men have tried to regulate and organize apart from and without God. The result has been that modern society is distinguished by great material progress unmatched by similar progress in the sphere of morality. Because of this there has also been a weakening of spiritual values, and from this there springs the search, more or less exclusively, for worldly pleasures, which advancing technology so easily provides for all.

Twice in these few lines the key word "technology" has been used: it is no longer possible to describe the modern world without using it. Man in the second half of the twentieth century is technological man; to use terminology suited both to the language of the Church and that of the natural sciences, *homo technicus* ("technological man"). Even if a man of natural melancholy who wants to live away from his fellows retreats to live among the most remote savages of Amazonia or New Guinea—"there will always be solitude on earth for those worthy of it," said de l'Isle Adam—yet his solitude can now be little more than imaginary. It would not involve any essentially individual originality. No iron curtain, no ocean, no prohibition, can halt the advance of automation. We are all fixed, pinned down, technologically by huge organizations. Materially speaking, every nation, and within each nation every individual, is today affected, won over or threatened by the behaviour patterns or the products of one and the same civilization, by the rules and the ambitions of one and the same conformity.

It is, it seems, only to be expected that a great many Christian writers should have followed one another in dealing with a problem as serious as this and as difficult, and one capable of being developed in so many contradictory ways. It is equally obvious that each of them, leaving aside any intellectual eccentricities, will have attempted to define the terms of the problem and to explain it in the light of his own personal experience. Such personal differences are inevitable and essential—*in dubiis libertas:* none of the theologians in the Council should be replaced by a robot.

In preparing to write this book, I have profited greatly from reading the works of such other writers. Can I hope to have added anything new? For such is the normal hope and the obligation of a writer. I have attempted to do so by freeing myself from a purely French context and extending my interest and sympathy to all countries of the world. If

France has rightly been called (with a question mark, it is true) a "mission territory", does not the same name belong to the whole earth? Consider a few facts which make one wonder whether the apostolic forces of the Church ought not to be redeployed: in Rio de Janeiro there is a parish of forty thousand souls in the care of one seventy-year-old priest; in Ruanda is a mission station where, of twenty-one thousand Christians who wanted to go to confession and communion in Holy Week only one-third could do so, because there were not enough priests.

Nor is this irrelevant: this is the very heart of the matter. Surely the sudden population explosion in Brazil must be brought into relation with technical progress? And surely automation, which fosters materialist ideologies and tends to produce a stereotyped idea of man, is at the same time and thereby a factor which might militate against vocations to the priesthood?

There are nowadays doctors who shrug their shoulders when they hear mention of alcoholism. The term, they say, corresponds to no scientific reality, and it is mere mental laziness to use it so lightly and generally. But the same reproach cannot be cast against us if we find the influence of technology in contemporary social phenomena or in the minds of contemporary individuals. We no longer need to inquire whether many men do not in their thinking become so overshadowed by its power that they treat it either as a universal panacea or as the root of all evil. I can at least say that its influence is felt everywhere. To establish this I do not need to mention interplanetary rockets: in London or New York, do we not all breathe the air of technology? Are not our educational syllabuses designed by experts, by technologists? Are not all our traffic regulations similarly designed by experts? And so on: I could go on giving examples.

Before I unfold the various senses of the word "technology", and state in which sense I intend generally to use it, I must emphasize that throughout this book I have tried to keep the problem, which concerns the difficulties of and the opportunities for the Christian faith in this technological world, quite separate from another problem, which deserves attention but which must be kept distinct, which is that of the attitude of modern science towards religion. I would not claim to have succeeded altogether; that is probably not possible. Technology is the child of science—often a degenerate child, but always bearing some resemblance to its parent. If my subject is technology, I shall be bound, sooner or later, to trespass into the domain of science. I have tried to keep such trespass within limits; for if the problems overlap, they are nevertheless distinct. It is possible, even likely, that a research scientist sleeps in the heart of the housewife who turns the button of her radio to fill the house with the same noise as everyone else, while she uses her vacuum cleaner; but the odds are long against this scientist ever awakening. Not all men are called to make or improve technological inventions, but all men, wherever they may be, are nowadays bound to use them or to suffer from them. It is on this that our searchlight must shine most brightly, even if the mental mechanisms thus shown up are bound to appear less brilliant than those of the physicist or biologist in his laboratory. A man in a white laboratory coat, holding a test tube up before his eyes, surrounded by delicate and complicated apparatus—such is the popular image of the scientist, the "cover-boy" of ordinary people. But ordinary people also were made in the image of God, and we must guard against treating them as mere accessories. The disciples of Christ were called "the salt of the earth"; and he, preaching to the masses, had no special regard for any élite. The scribes and the Pharisees, who may stand in a general way for the intellectuals of the time, would have liked to get him to themselves so as to be able to denigrate him more thoroughly, but he always spoke to and for every man.

While working on this book I have been struck by the readiness with which so many Catholic intellectuals hail the achievements of technology. And I must admit that sometimes I have been worried by this. Perhaps my friends in Christ have been affected in an obscure way—and in all good faith—by a kind of false shame as they look back at what they might judge to have been a regrettable slowness on the part of the Church to adapt herself; and they have perhaps consequently protested too loudly their own lack of any jealousy of technology, which they hold never to have been necessary. Now enthusiasm is no doubt a very good thing: but only, as Péguy said, for a good cause—hopeless, it may be, but good. It does not seem certain that tremendous technological "progress" is such a cause. Certainly we should put ourselves at the service of mankind; certainly the improvements in man's material well-being made possible by technological discovery are essential to mankind and to man's religious life; but this does not simply and necessarily imply that the Christian should kow-tow before technology or think it all-powerful.

May one not rightly be astonished to find in an otherwise excellent book: "Interplanetary space henceforth belongs to man. The moon no longer has any secrets for him, now that he has photographed its other side . . ."? Now that this is the general impression nowadays, that this is how many people look at it, and that Christians must take it seriously and think about it, all this is true: but need one support and even confirm such an opinion? Again, ought one not to be shocked by such a statement as this: "It must be admitted that it is not prayer, but the progress of medicine and of economics which has freed mankind from epidemics and from famine"? Is this not to cut too easily and lightly into the domain of God? Does the phrase, "I nursed him, God

cured him", now offend because of too much humility?
When a preacher, before asking for money for this or that
cause, asks for the prayers of his congregation, ought one to
say to him: "Get on with it, that's a waste of time"?

We all, I suppose, laughed heartily, or at any rate smiled
broadly, when we read Huxley's *Brave New World*. We
laughed with the greater calm because we felt ourselves to be
fore-armed by our Christian truths against the possibilities
of such a gloomy future. On principle, Christians need not
be afraid. To those who grumble, "Mankind is mad! The
way things are going there will be five thousand million men
on this earth by the end of the century!" the Christian
cheerfully replies, "So what?" After all, they can quote
quite serious economists who say that if agricultural economists improve the techniques of farming, the earth could
easily support twenty-seven thousand million human beings.
It is so large a number the imagination boggles; but let it
stand—nothing in our Christian faith is against it: the love
of God for men has not fixed the number.

But is it unreasonable to laugh scornfully at any figure
that may be given, as being seen at once to be too small?
If the rate of increase continues naturally, as there is no
reason to think it will not, even if it slows up, in five or six
centuries there will be a million millions of living men, and
in a thousand or two thousand years there will be a thousand
million million. Suppose a Christian says this; is he not then
engaging, in all sincerity, in a sort of competition with
agnostic scientists to see who can forecast the highest
figures? Let us agree with him, all the same, and then let us
say that if his forecasts come true the men of that future
time must settle their own problems. Let us restrict ourselves to ours. To the technological humour of the intellectual who proposes cramming millions more people into the
square mile, let us reply with a mystical humour which, in
that area of events which are near enough for the reason to

guess at beyond this present moment, explicitly sets the *parousia*, the second coming of God on the earth. It must have a big question mark after it, of course, for the sake of common-sense; but let it be postulated. Could it not be just as legitimate to expect the *parousia* as to expect a fantastic growth in the population of the world? And as a great saint has taught, the best way to prepare for God's second coming is to attend to today's tasks. One of these is to provide the conditions for a good and harmonious life for the overflow of humanity to come, recognizing that that task is not to be thought of only in material terms, and that it is not the only task we have to attend to, using up all our resources.

It is easy to criticize. I shall not be kept free of error simply by my intention that my examination of the potentialities of technology shall be a cool and deliberate one. I hope that the reader will correct me, and forgive me, if I put forward anything unreasonable. Like all those who have gone before me, I am venturing into a difficult country, of shifting features, which has not yet been accurately mapped by theology; there are no roads, only rough tracks, and sometimes there are no footbridges to cross streams which are often foul, and one must jump, with the risk of falling in and getting filthy. To journey into the modern world, which is all round us and seems to fill our vision, is to journey into night.

So many contemporary judgements put forward are neat and striking, but only half true. The technologist has been defined as an expert who knows more and more about less and less. Very neat: but it would be as fair to describe him as one who knows less and less about more and more. The contemporary "specialist" (who is a sort of second-line expression of *homo technicus:* the technocrat comes higher in the hierarchy) generally obtains what knowledge he has of disciplines other than his own through the medium of digests, television, magazines, and so on—a "third-hand" culture.

If one has to be very careful about distinctions in the comparatively simple realm of statements about the material world, *a fortiori* one is in great danger, where moral issues are involved, of fumbling about for ever without getting anywhere. We shall cling to the marvellous phrase of Fr M.-D. Chenu: "The technological civilization of today is a missionary territory." This means that the Church, in her concern for the salvation of the world, must now apply herself to saving the civilization which has spread across the world. But before it can be saved it must first be brought into the light and made clearly and accurately known. Like all missionary territories, it is as yet hardly explored or mapped out.

I have challenged the truth of the idea that the suppression of epidemics and of famine may be attributed simply to the advances made in medicine and economics. When I read the words, I was at once brought up sharply by them. But I was fairly sure that the author would, a few pages later, himself take up the idea again and correct it, carefully and properly: "Man is never purely and simply a creator, is never the absolute origin of his own works." And then he would introduce and analyse the double dependence of all human action, on man himself and on God. In the same way, when Fr Chenu writes: "Through his technological skill, man enters explicitly into the making of the world, and legitimately claims this power", we should not immediately suspect him of an unfortunate tendency to make a god of man. Two pages later, he introduces the necessary complement: "The more man takes possession of nature, the more mysterious nature becomes, for in being humanized it partakes of the mystery of man." All this means that in such a delicate matter, when they are elaborating the doctrine of the Church, her greatest thinkers are themselves involved in expressions which warp their thought. We must not allow ourselves to judge them on such expressions, because we can know what they really think from other things they say. The fact that a speaker drops his glasses half way through a paragraph does not detract from the beauty of his argument (if any).

But this somewhat off-hand indulgence must not be interpreted as meaning that I have no regard for the truth, one and distinct as it is. I may speak of language as did Aesop, calling it at once the loveliest and the most dreadful, the most useful and the most dangerous gift of man. Moralists frequently judge automation in much the same way.

This being said, I hope that the main thread of this book will not be too obscure. If it happens that I can be accused of producing contradictions between one paragraph and another, then I hope to be able to swing the tiller over quickly and get back on to course before I have gone very far adrift. My object is not to impose my opinions on the reader, but to stimulate his own thoughts and dreams. The vast problem tackled in this little book, which is one of the essential concerns of the Ecumenical Council, will not be solved—if at all—simply by the intellectual skill or the spiritual holiness of the theologians assembled in Rome. Still less will it be solved by the good intentions of any writer. For a task of such magnitude the collaboration of all men, in their practical experience, is needed.

Perhaps I myself am wide of the mark; who can say? My plan for this book prevents my expressing my conclusions here. But perhaps I could say now—since I have made it clear that I will not kow-tow to technology—what I hope. There is a fourth possibility for the future besides the *parousia*, besides a dreadful war which would annihilate nine-tenths of mankind and reduce the rest to the life of cavemen, and besides a "population explosion" with a corresponding increase in all forms of madness. It is still possible that we may enter on an age of relative calm and reflection: not a golden age, nor simply an age of transition, but a real and normal continuation, a period of clarification and of drawing things together.

CHAPTER I

TERMS OF REFERENCE:

TECHNOLOGY

Technology is a portmanteau word, applicable to many different things. It has already been assimilated into everyday speech, and has been so for a long time; so much so that it is often grossly misused. So we need to clarify its meaning, since there is a great difference between technique and technology, and between technologies used in the plural and Technology.

In a vague and ordinary sense, which is perhaps the first that comes to mind, a technology is a set of methods devised as a whole to obtain some particular result. It follows that every field of human activity should have its appropriate technology. As each science is applied, it will give birth to, or stimulate the creation of, a certain number of technologies. For the rules of cricket or the disposal of household refuse, for fly-fishing or for electronic engineering, for any skill, in fact, there are, in common parlance, "experts" or "specialists"; that is, men who possess a certain kind of knowledge and can use it knowing what they are doing.

The Bible tells us that man began by giving names to all that there was. This was the first moment of his power, this giving of names, which already suggests a "technological" view of the world. Then, strictly in conformity with the divine will—"Increase and multiply and fill the earth, and make it yours" (or with the great promises, "Ask and you shall receive, knock and it shall be opened unto you", and so on)—man sought to use all that he had thus named and classified. This is what, continuing since the beginning, has brought into being all the development of the different technologies.

Now this is a summary and symbolic account of it, we may admit; and the work of naming things has gone on all the time that their use has been developed. This sounds simple: but it is a matter of putting technology in its proper place, which is very high in the scale. When man was described as *homo faber* ("man the maker"), it was not just that he was being granted a simple vocation to be a medieval craftsman, fiddling at his small daily labours in sight of the passers-by in Tailors Street or Smith Street; nor that he could potter around his suburban villa doing odd jobs. It was intended to mark in a single and simple word one of his sovereign qualities. Man, created by God in his image and for his glory, has this power of the *maker* in his blood. There is no pejorative implication in this, as there is in the last analysis in the Greek *polymetis*, the epithet of Odysseus "of many ruses". *Homo faber* is above simple resourcefulness, cleverness at getting out of trouble. He is exercising a function taught him by God, he is continuing God's work: a reflection from God lights him up in his work.

The harmonious and proper complement of knowledge is "know-how". When we studied logic, we all learned, without worrying about it, *bene scire, scire per causas*, that is, real knowledge must include knowledge of causes. But *homo faber* adds to the minutiae of theory the confident verification of his technology. Without knowing it, he puts into practice the slogan, *bene scire, scire per consequentias* or *per applicationes*: it is in applying it that he pays homage to that pure knowledge without which his applications could not exist. It is his own way of serving the truth: to show it to us at the level of, embodied in, as it were, material things. And clearly in his own fashion he remains true to the spirit of the Gospel words: "A tree is recognized by its fruits."

Homo faber: clearly a good fellow, in ordinary language. He is not simply man as able to work in wood or stone or other materials, but man as able to rationalize all his acts and skills and to teach them. Along with the instinct to make things goes that to give and to share.

Although we can only reconstruct the story in a very sketchy way, we can understand well enough what an extraordinary event it was in the history of man when, after much trial and error, or perhaps as a sudden discovery, the first flame produced by a human hand was followed by the careful recapitulation of the series of movements producing that same result. The present generation has already forgotten the enthusiasm with which it greeted the first sputnik in orbit. If a country sends up an untried rocket and then fails to recover its pretty little capsule in the shrunken immensities of the ocean, men complain that they are bunglers, as if rockets should now be as easily managed as fairground air-rifles. But perhaps this blasé indifference, which daily swallows its diet of super-inventions, fits us best of all to reconsider the difficulties of the earliest beginnings, and to understand that in its own age the spread of the conquest of fire was a much more important and sensational event than, in the recent past, was the commercial utilization —at a price, of course—of electric light.

Whatever aspect of the Promethean genius of man one wishes to stress—boldness, tenacity, cleverness, the gift of imitation or intelligence, and so on—the conquest of fire deserves to be called a technical achievement, or even a technological achievement. It is a technology of bare hands, with no special tools, but none the less it is already aiming at the transformation of matter for the benefit of man.

Could we perhaps go further, and because of its extra-ordinary usefulness to the ages that were to come, set down to the credit of Technology, that imperial monarch Technology, the humble implement used to produce fire? I do not think so.

I must stress that my reply is not dictated by any contempt for the past. I am not at all inclined, because of the increasing pace of development both in the number and noisiness of human inventions, to despise the tremendous labours of all the generations that have gone before. Because one likes one's own times and wants them to be more friendly, more united, one is not bound to suggest that they are the only age of genius and that the rest of history is not worth a fig. The flow of events is unbroken ever since the Creation, and the solidarity of mankind at any one time clearly implies the solidarity of all mankind all down the centuries. The universe is indeed much older than man, but in comparison with the individual's lifetime man himself is no mere lad.

But even if painting did not begin with Picasso, nor music with the dodecaphonists, nor architecture with Le Corbusier, nor even nuclear explosions with the atom bomb, it still seems impossible not to draw a clear distinction between *homo faber* and *homo technicus*. It is true that the latter could never have existed without the other, and that he is of no greater worth before God. Yet his appearance is an event of very great importance, and his proliferation, with his awareness of his rights and powers, must make psychologists and sociologists, Christian and others, reconsider their view of the world. Surely we may now speak, without any exaggeration, of a Technological Age (following an age of speculation and experiment?) just as we can distinguish in the darkness of man's earlier history a Neolithic or a Bronze Age.

The Technological Age: the term is not too strong.
Remember the words of *Humanae salutis* we have already
quoted: "At a time when mankind is at a turning-point,
entering a new age. . . ." These are the words, not of some
Hyde Park Corner speaker, nor of some politician making a
speech, but of a pope, after prayer and reflection. Observe
how careful is the phrasing, and how wise: it cannot yet be
asserted that mankind, all mankind, has entered the Technological Age, but only that it is preparing to do so. But
whether it is completed or not, the revolution produced by
the development of technology is under way. Even if we go on
believing that man does not change in his essential nature—
and that is an act of faith which is becoming more and more
difficult to make—at least the behaviour of men in the world
is changing with ever-increasing rapidity. All the brakes
seem to be off; the age now beginning is different from preceding eras in that it seems not to care about consolidating
itself in a time of rest and of flowering. True to its constant
mobility, the Technological Age is seen to be an Age of
Variation, of Perpetual Change. The minds of some thinkers
have been given to analysing what is happening, and the
idea of the acceleration of technology has been produced.
When we call it an "age of speed" we ought not to think
only of jet aircraft and fast cars, but also of this constant
renewal of our "universe".

We must go further in our analysis: when we speak of
constant renewal we are not falling into any kind of "catas-
trophism". The reader already knows, we hope, how difficult
it would be for us to be united with other men in brotherly
love if we criticized their successive civilizations from
beginning to end. By making plain the extent of the revolution which is now beginning we are surely putting ourselves
immediately in a better position to attack a certain kind of
pessimism. A priest aboard a ship that is foundering does
not waste time exclaiming that it should never have left

harbour, that the voyage was mad: nor should we Christians
of the twentieth century lament the chances squandered
since the Fall—oh! if only Cleopatra had been a good
mother! If only Henry VIII had controlled his passions!
If only Stalin had listened to the teachings of Pius XII!
Let us live in this our world, for which, in its present order
or even disorder, was shed the blood of Christ.

The first man was a technologist without knowing it. The
technical advances made by man since the beginning have
been countless, and they have been made in the most diverse
fields. Among them are great and wonderful successes
which one who would be objective cannot ignore or contest
without going gravely wrong. What if the Tower of Babel
was a failure: we should look at that strange story impar-
tially. Have we not experienced quite as serious and even
more vast failures of collective organization in the two
world wars which have drenched our modern generations
in blood? Yet even then, while they hurled themselves
against one another, some modern nations doubled their
industrial potential, and in the fervour of the conflict the
excited imaginations of their scientists discovered the most
astonishing inventions. Whether we think of the pyramids of
Egypt, of the temples of Ang-kor, of Socrates' "midwifery",
of the Roman legion or the Roman road, of the medieval
cathedral, or the leaning tower of Pisa, or the châteaux of
the Loire, of the Suez or Panama canals, or of the anticipa-
tions made by Jules Verne, surely in all times and places we
can find methods and organizations, undertakings and
products which show clearly the technological skill of *homo
faber*. He has always been able to conceive and work out an
idea; to estimate what materials, what machines, and what
labour force will be needed and then get them all together;
to organize and coordinate the labours of many different
groups of workmen according to a single plan; to be the one
who can bring out of unorganized confusion, despite the

recalcitrance of matter, the triumphant realization of an idea.

The older technology may have been workmanlike and empirical, but it was none the less technology. Good judges claim that the palace of Versailles and its gardens were never as fine and beautiful under the kings of France as they are now. That may be so, but on the other hand, we cannot forget or ignore the brilliance, never since equalled, of medieval stained-glass windows. The older technology was the forerunner of our own. Already it was claiming to be indispensable to men, and long ago some enlightened spirits protested against a factotum imposing its presence everywhere. It is this which makes de Musset's young dreamer Fantasio exclaim: "What a wretched creature man is! He has to play the violin for ten years to become a passable musician, he has to learn how to paint, or how to groom his horse, or even how to make an omelette!" Poor Fantasio! What would you say to our "sex education"?

It would be futile to try to date the change from *homo faber* to *homo technicus*, especially since the change occurred, or began to occur, in different countries at different times. There are, however, a few odd signs pointing to its happening. In Britain, the polytechnics of the eighteen-eighties were followed by the founding of the Imperial College of Science and Technology in 1907. Although the word is at least as old as the early seventeenth century in English, this was its first use in the title of an educational institution in England. But it had been used forty-six years earlier in the United States, in the Massachusetts Institute of Technology, and that had itself been preceded by other technical colleges, the earliest being the Rensselaer Polytechnic Institute, which began in 1824. In spite of this, and despite also the fairly common use of the word all through the nineteenth century in its modern sense, "Technology" does not appear in the fourteenth edition (1946) of the *Encyclopaedia Britannica*, though "Technocracy", as a political theory, does.

Technology was defined at an international congress of cyberneticians in Namur in 1958, by Louis Couffignal: "Technology is generally opposed to science, as consisting of a succession of actions accomplishing a particular practical end. The description of that succession of actions is a dialectical model of the action, the programme for it." Now I may as well admit that I began by objecting to these words; they appeared to me to hide and uphold, under their flat expression, a false idea. But I was wrong. Much that they say can be retained. Brought together with another current definition of technology, as the collection of processes allowing the methodical application of discoveries to the needs and projects of man, Couffignal's definition, insisting as it does on the close relationship between technology and action, makes it possible for us to take a good step forward in the discussion and to understand that independently of all technologies now existing or to come, there already exists, in men's minds, Technology, just like that. It is extremely difficult to go on thinking that we are only dealing with a myth.

As I write this, I have before me a summary of a pastoral letter published by Cardinal Richaud. Here are two quotations: "Need we still stress that the logic of the Church's apostolic work presupposes that all the living forces of its apostolate should regularly be organized within the framework of units recognized by the hierarchy and directed by their representatives? . . . Every modern activity necessarily implies a certain technique and a certain organization and direction." Perhaps the phrase "a certain technique" still betrays some hesitation in the use of the word; but we are nevertheless dealing with expertise, techniques, technology. And the fact that this reference occurs in a context dealing with the dilution of the clergy and the organizing of the apostolic efforts of God's representatives makes it particularly revealing.

For the relief of all those—priests, writers, compilers of dictionaries—who try in good faith to define in all its complexity one of the principal—if not *the* principal—concepts of modern times, it must be said that those "in the trade", or those who seem most entitled to be so called, for no one nowadays is completely cut off from technology, allow themselves in practice some disturbing contradictions and vaguenesses. It is impossible to establish on any rational grounds a clear distinction between "scientists" and "technologists": an ex-student of a college of technology with a diploma may find himself doing the job of a research scientist, while a man with a university degree in science or engineering may find himself classified as a technologist. Here, we need not criticize such anomalies; we have to consider their implications. In some circumstances, the word "technologist" can be used in a complimentary way to mean a man with a certain skill and "know-how"; in others, particularly when it is a matter of establishing those distinctions at an administrative level which are the source, along with inequalities in the way men are treated, of differences in social standing, the same word can take on a pejorative colouring. It seems to have collected some of the old contempt surrounding the phrase "manual worker". Even if it is not intended to imply that a technologist is a "worker", it does suggest that his life is limited to materials and machines, and that the broader perspectives of industry are beyond him.

Yet there is scarcely a position in any of the industrial concerns of our time that is not to some degree technological, that does not in some way declare the necessity for technology. In the various services of manufacture, research, prospecting, commerce, and administration, and in the medical and social services, it is everywhere necessary to use complicated machines or apparatus, everywhere the telephone rings and the typewriter clacks, everywhere there are files, minutes, card-indexes and reports, at every level there is the problem of administration and of organized cooperation in the achieving of a common task, in fulfilling a set programme in a given time.

Technology has, in fact, vastly extended its field of action since *homo faber* first appeared, since the invention of the spinning-wheel and the hand-forge. Its products now range from the extraordinary complexity of a great oil refinery to the quietly purring vacuum cleaner that removes the dust from the carpet or the upholstery, from a nuclear reactor to an ordinary rotary date-stamp, from minute transistor radios to can-openers, from H-bombs to Elvis Presley records. All matter now comes within its scope, and every man is now involved, directly or indirectly. Perhaps the material forces put at his service by technology influence his behaviour and hence his psychology; or perhaps technology will take him also into its field of operation. It is conceivable: if technology is not—some would say, "not yet"—all-powerful, yet already it affects everything and everybody. When Laloup defined it as "any natural method of acting on matter with a physical end in view" he was wrong: there are already technologies of man, not only of his body, but of his mind, concerned with his deepest "motivations", his desires, his inclinations.

When man relieved himself of physical fatigue by letting a machine do the work for him, or when he made a machine to do something he could not do himself, he did not notice at the time that he would one day have to pay for his conquests, that he was mechanizing himself, that he was surrounding himself with a proliferating mass of material "assistants"—machines for discovering, for preparing, for collecting, for thinking, even—that although a machine is a proper symbol of technology, so also is a pile of papers.

The invention of machine-tools marks an important stage in what we may call the "humanizing progress" of technology. Next came the birth and rapid development of automation, and then the development of all the industrial applications of nuclear fission. The layman who sees for the first time the working of an automatic pilot, or of a rocket missile, or of a nuclear power-station, certainly, when he thinks about it, wonders at the thought and work and the calculations of men which have gone into the making of these mechanical masterpieces, these marvellous machines; but he cannot help also wondering about the immense scope for invention, for initiative, which man thus abandons to these objects, these machines, intended to take his place, to be his "assistants". True, he remains their master; he does not abdicate his domination of the world in their favour. But he does invite them to cooperate with him. He accepts the responsibility for all those actions which are theirs and his and, materially regarded, more theirs than his, and includes them indiscriminately under the general heading of human activity.

At this point, it might not be irrelevant to express some anxiety. Not that man should be reproached with over-estimating the value of technology. If I deride, it is without malice, for in and beyond technology I can see well enough that man is pursuing, in a more or less confused manner, quests essential to his nature, quests for Order and Truth, with capital letters. In such a pursuit, mistakes cannot be avoided. But in considering automation, or nuclear fission, we must not simply be weakly indulgent, but must also have regard to the darker aspects of the picture. At present, automation is not benefiting from the rapid progress of technology, since it has in most countries been artificially held back, because of the fear now felt by specialists concerning the magnitude of the social changes it could bring about. But how long can it be so held back? In this field works the influence, for good or ill, of the technocrats. Who are they? All those whom one might suppose belong to this class deny it vigorously; yet the class exists. They are not simply the technologists, but rather their masters, those who mediate between them and Technology. The technology of the technocrats is that which governs and animates all the others. Theirs is the relentless search for material resources, for methods of exploitation, for new needs to satisfy. It is they who deny the world any time to draw breath. They are the human agents of that accelerating progess which today seems to be the essential characteristic of man's collective physical and intellectual life. And if the capitalist world has its technocrats, the Communist world must also have its own.

As for nuclear fission, no one can be ignorant of the terrible dangers mankind now faces because of its applications. I must try to write of it calmly. Before I began this book, I tried to survey the question, by rereading various articles and by going over again all the recent arguments; and I am left with a bitter taste in the mouth. It is difficult to appreciate the distinction between "clean" and "dirty" bombs, or the false philosophy of those who assure us that the world would not be annihilated by a nuclear war: its victims would only be counted in hundreds of millions. After the Second World Conference on the Peaceful Uses of Nuclear Energy at Vienna in 1958, a large number of scientists, belonging to twenty-two nations, who had already met twice before for similar discussions, gathered at Kitzbühel. A communiqué was issued, the first paragraph of which ("The necessity to put an end to war") contained the following declarations: "We meet at a time when it has become clear that the development of nuclear weapons has made man capable of annihilating civilization and of destroying himself. The scientists who have taken part in our discussions are unanimous in considering that a total atomic war would be a world catastrophe on an unprecedented scale. In our

opinion, defence against an atomic attack is extremely
difficult. A blind confidence in defensive measures could
even contribute towards the unleashing of such a war."
When we read this, how can we not agree with Fr Daniélou
when he says: "Technological man is afraid. He is afraid
because he now disposes of such forces that cosmic catas-
trophes, of which he could be the instrument, have now
become perfectly possible."

But there are other collective fears, less spectacular, but
equally serious, produced by the advance of technology in
the fields of man's speculative thought and intellectual life.
Man, through technology, and Technology, through man,
have now acquired, as well as the power to destroy wholly
or in part the earth and its peoples, the power to destroy or
change man's nature. This is a power apart from all the
changes in the whole background of modern life which may
in the long run affect his nature. To be precise, certain techniques, which represent as it were an advancing flank of
Technology, its darling children, have as their aim action on
the mind of man. They have already, in a discreet way,
begun to influence our daily lives. With psychological tests
and psychoanalysis, the ordinary man generally ends up
having suffered such things to some small degree. There is,
of course, a very great difference between the mental tortures
practised by political police and psychological tests as they
are used in all sorts of spheres, but it is only a difference of
degree, and some techniques of this kind can properly be
described as "brain-washing".

Huxley's *Brave New World* made all its readers of my
generation laugh a good deal, with a delight that was
unmixed. It was described by literary critics as a novel of the
future, and none of us took seriously such unbridled fantasy:
it seemed to us so far removed from reality. Yet it was a
novel of the future: one after the other Huxley's imaginings
have become a part of our real, everyday world. Did we

laugh at the idea of teaching little children during their sleep by means of gramophone records? My friends, take back those smiles: look at this advertisement from an American magazine: "LEARN WHEN YOU SLEEP. Use your recorder, phonograph or amazing new ELECTRONIC EDUCATOR, . . . endless tape-recorder. Fascinating, educational . . . Details, catalog free. Write 'Sleep-learning Research Assn.' ".

How simple it all is! All day, while you work, drive or simply relax, all you want from the radio is pleasant music. At night, while you sleep, you follow a course in Chinese language or in political economy. It is difficult not to believe that such a life would, at least in the long run, change the nature of man.

"Oh, to think such terrible things happen! To think there are such monsters!" So sighs the housewife reading the latest crime story in her newspaper. She does not reflect that she might herself, perhaps, find in her own life the elements of just "such terrible things". When she hears on the radio an account of the methods used in a camp where political prisoners are "re-educated", she sighs again. She does not dream that when her housework is done and she goes shopping, she more than once follows the instructions given her in the advertisements telling her to buy this or that, which control, without her being aware of it, her actions and her words.

Technology has created electronic brains which seem to make machines more like men. From another aspect, has it not also been busy making men more like machines, making man as automatic? Is the reaction of the 'bus-driver who stops at the red lights so different from that of the pick-up arm which, when the record is finished, lifts itself and returns to the rest position?

It is not altogether impossible that there is a certain element of bluff in the present prestige of technology. The astonishing facility with which man uses technical language to give himself the impression that he is penetrating reality, delving into the secrets of the world, has been frequently stressed by philosophers. Is it not a strange abuse to call a machine that needs a driver an *automobile*? Today, there are remote-controlled machines which can do without a driver, it is true, but can one say that the remote control works all on its own? As we have already said, "technology" is a portmanteau word. Technology has wormed its way into everything, and it is now often given a part to play which it cannot in fact play. The realm and the influence of technology overlap many others: those of science, which it has often attempted to replace but which always directs and leads it; those of industry and of labour, of finance and commerce, even of fashion. Whether it is quite justifiable or not, a "presence" such as that of technology, which ceaselessly makes itself felt in the lives of all men, and which casts its shadow over all man's decisions, is a fundamental part of his mental make-up. "At a time when mankind is at a turning-point, entering a new age. . . ." We can still hear John XXIII's words. Man, or a certain number of men who more or less legitimately claim to speak and act in his name and for his good, have acquired an extraordinary power over the material world, and are beginning to acquire the same power over man himself; and these powers are rapidly increasing.

Through a thousand difficulties—some of which at least are spurious—and under the very real threat of catastrophe, a civilization is taking shape. It claims to increase and to go on increasing the powers of man. By putting the potentialities of the material world more and more at his disposal, it seems to seek to bring out of Everyman the Superman—that Superman whom philosophers have always thought of as a very rare spirit indeed—and to seek to set up Everyman as master of himself and of his own happiness.

This is not exaggeration. The contemporary "technocrat"

behaves like an enlightened despot. Whether he intends them to or not, his actions point towards a world in which those men whose needs and reactions he now governs and arranges shall one day feel that they exert a full collective authority over a world without riddles.

But the Christian Church has something to say. "Wait and see" is not her attitude. Nothing that happens in the mind and spirit of man is foreign to her. She must think it out and take her stand, confronted as she is by an enterprise which may be—and none can deny it *a priori*—rich and full of promise, but which is certainly rushing ahead too fast and is full of dangers. We must see whether the christianization of this more or less blind progress is not possible. The Church has often enough turned the energies of barbarians to peaceful ends.

But in order to prepare for this confrontation and, it may be, this reconciliation, Christian belief must itself first attempt a real self-analysis.

CHAPTER II

TERMS OF REFERENCE:

FAITH

By this short English word, which lends itself so readily to wordplay, we understand both a disposition of the mind and a collection of beliefs; nor is it always profitable to distinguish the two meanings.

It used to be the right thing to do, when one began to speak of an "organized harmony", to shrug one's shoulders and ask: "Organized? By whom?" And when faith was mentioned, some would indulge in the same sort of mockery: "Faith in what?" But that was the wrong question. Before the mind begins to conceptualize and codify its belief, faith is already there. It is in its essence a movement of trusting acceptance, a certain expectation of being blessed by an annunciation. All Christians can find it in their childhood, while only gradually and later do they learn the dogmas of their religion. The soul of man is always ready to receive the truth which comes to it, which it hopes for and which it needs.

Taking our inspiration from one of the most beautiful parables in the Gospel, we may say that faith is understood both of the seed that falls on the earth and of the good earth which receives that seed. Before we can know the object of our belief, we already in some way "believe".

So far as one can isolate this extremely brief moment, which only takes on its full meaning as it passes to the next stage, it is clear that this hidden readiness to believe is quite different from credulity. It is not a willingness to accept any story one is told. If a mind becomes muddled and confused by superstitions, it is because other forces, both within and without, have already changed and warped the normal tendencies of its nature. It must rather be drawn towards that general desire for learning which is so strong in infancy and adolescence, and which is one of the most essential characteristics of our nature. We long to learn, for we are obscurely aware that these things can be understood. Faith, as a disposition of the mind, is seen as a thirst for learning and knowing the whole of the Truth, the final and complete Truth, in the light of which we can then understand the detail and the depths of our lives.

When theologians speak of an *anima naturaliter Christiana*, they properly stress, by the use of the adverb *naturaliter* sandwiched between the noun and its adjective, the agreement between the truths of the Christian faith and the deepest instincts of man's mind.

The religious psychologist who examines this need in the child to believe and to know soon discovers that he is not dealing with a vague potentiality only, and that the outlines of a certain content of faith can be seen beneath the apparent indistinctness. The need and the thirst for belief are even then a thirst and a need for belief in an invisible being beyond the world, a creator who governs the world with wisdom and goodness. Even when we can hardly yet walk, when our lips can scarcely pronounce properly a few small words—some names of persons or animals or concrete objects—even then there is in us a desire to believe in transcendence.

The Revelation in history and the Incarnation are later explained to us by others as facts which the mind cannot itself draw out of its own darkness; yet when the child first meets them, he feels that he recognizes them, not in their detail, certainly, but in their whole reality and truth. That God should be made man—that act of God's which seems incomprehensible to so many adults—shocks him not at all. Rather does he think of it as natural, as a supreme proof of the love of God for men, the generous kindness of God in giving to unbelievers and sceptics an opportunity to turn away from their doubts and their anxieties and their rejection.

But this natural basis is not enough. These marvellous beginnings of faith, which are already faith, do not yet make that faith Christian. They can, and do, issue in various religions. We frequently use the term "faith" in a wide sense to mean faith in transcendence, in an invisible creator God, and so on. All the same, we must recognize that for us the context, and the fulfilment of these great metaphysical ideas, in which we can see a sort of "common good" of the principal religions and of some individual systems of thought, is really Christianity.

In other words, I am not concerned here with the relations between technology and animism or spiritualism or theism or Islam or any religion other than Christianity. As I go along, I may go beyond the limits of Christianity—and I shall be delighted to have done so—but I do not seek to do so. And by Christianity is meant the Roman Catholic faith, which is the most widespread form.

The idea is simple and clear. One of the basic prayers of the Christian life is the "act of faith": in it the believer declares in a general way his firm belief in all the truths which God has revealed to us and which he teaches us through his Church. The essentials of these truths are seen in the Creed, which is also called a profession of faith, which is recited or sung at the end of the "Mass of the catechumens".

One would like to write: for the rest, open your catechisms. One could; and one could stop there. But then one's intellect would be, so to speak, very scantily furnished with Christian ideas. A deepening of all the articles of faith is, if not absolutely necessary, at least greatly to be desired. The catechism does not say: "No one is presumed ignorant of the faith." There are no booby-traps in a religion which looks to God for absolute justice. No: the Church ceaselessly tells us: "Instruct yourselves in the faith; have an enlightened faith."

To say of someone that he was *very* Christian, or *very* believing or *very* Catholic, might seem silly, for faith cannot be measured in cubic feet or pounds; yet the expression is not perhaps quite meaningless. In ancient China, a mandarin's rank in the hierarchy was fixed according to the number of written characters he knew. Even if there is nothing quite like this in the Catholic Church, it is nevertheless certain that her faithful are not all equally instructed in the truths of their faith, and that the Church today is making great efforts to teach them more.

The "act of faith" begins with a very significant adverb: "I *firmly* believe . . ." and goes on with a no less significant adjective: "*all* the truths . . . ". To believe is not simply to give lip-service to, nor to believe in half the dogmas plus one, nor even to believe in all the dogmas save one, but to believe utterly and deeply every one of the articles of the message. Scope and firmness of belief do really go together, though in some cases they may not seem to. The simple faith of the humble and ignorant poor can sometimes be shattering, like the simple little cross which once stood in place of signature for the illiterate. Surely there are little ones and humble ones and weak ones who share fully in the life of the Church and go to make up the Communion of Saints.

There is no need to qualify their praise. As there are many mansions in the house of the Father, so many different attitudes of faith may command our respect. In the utter submission of the ignorant no one is *a priori* entitled to sneer at dullness or idleness. The last sentence of the "act of faith", which all believers accept, be they university professors or

peasants, refers the belief of Christians expressly to a statement of trust in "God, who is the Sovereign Truth, who can
neither deceive nor be deceived". The Christian is not
asked to believe because he has found in his experience that
his beliefs are right, but, much more simply, and much less
intellectually, because he is a child of God.

Now it may be suspected that there must be a serious
conflict between technology and the Christian faith, now
that we have got to this point. Can this spirit of submission
to God and to the Church in the quest for religious truth, on
which all truth depends, be reconciled otherwise than
artificially with the spirit of sceptical control and watchful-
ness? Can the two priorities, of spiritual and physical well-
being, be brought together?

But wait: the problem is not one of abstract ideas, but
is enacted in the heart of man; it cannot be so briefly sum-
marized, so caricatured.

First, in the faith of the centurion ("say but the word")
we have perhaps an example of the ideal; and equally
ideal, perhaps, is the return to the simplicity of childhood—"Believe me, unless you become like little children
again. . . ." Again we may say that there are many mansions
in the Father's house. Beneath that faith which requires no
proof, which, as it were, signs agreement without reading
the terms, as part of the order of things since the beginning
of the world, there is a faith which allows itself time for
scrutiny and reflection, which judges one thing after another,
and builds up a structure gradually—a faith no less sincere,
and still agreeable to God. "Thou hast learned to believe,
Thomas, because thou hast seen me . . ."—there is a note of
regret in Christ's voice, for he expected more of his disciple,
but there is no blame—"Blessed are those who have not seen,
and yet have learned to believe." Indeed, the former have
given us the example of a higher faith. But the others, with
their more earthbound souls, are still men of good will, and

to the end of time St Thomas, who may be regarded as their leader, will still be honoured as one of the Twelve.

But although we must be careful not to reduce the Christian faith to a single type, we must at the same time insist on the fact that the centurion's faith was accompanied by an intellectual process. It was a total faith, expressed in an unreserved acceptance, but it was supported by an argument: "I too know what it is to obey authority; I have soldiers under me, and I say, Go, to one man, and he goes, or, Come, to another, and he comes, or, Do this, to my servant, and he does it. Even I, who am only a man, exercise some authority; how can you, who are God, not be almighty?" This Gospel story, which some commentators have treated as a sign of friendship towards the military (the famous alliance of the sword and the aspergillum), has a profound general meaning. "There is no authority save from God": but man's authority is exercised in many fields, and besides man's command over other men there is also, no less striking, his authority over the material world. Man's thought can recognize God's plan in the natural elements of the world, and feel itself confounded by what it sees. The centurion's humble faith thus seems in no way contradictory to the realist faith of the technologist or research scientist, to which it is in any case much nearer than it is to the simple faith attributed to the charcoal-burner.

"Rash soul, wouldst thou be assured that faith without deeds to show has no life in it?" It is a pressing and disturbing question, beyond doubt; but there is another which is no less essential: can that faith which is not cultivated and deepened be truly lively? But perhaps this second question is merely a particular case of the first. Among other signs of sincerity and liveliness, for faith, there must be this cultivation and deepening.

The living Church affirms this, through the popes, through its theologians and through its moral teachings: as far as he possibly can the believer is bound to go on endlessly finding out more about his faith. That faith, we repeat, is not to be reduced, ought not to be reduced, to a happy disposition of the mind. It must possess some content. "Go and *teach* all nations." How can a too ignorant man prepare himself worthily for the sacrament of penance? Now, in the twentieth century, when all peoples without exception are voluntarily undergoing great sacrifices to raise the level of their general culture and their technological culture, the Christian must carefully try to study his faith and be well informed about it. Nor is this an attitude born of fear or mistrust; fear and mistrust would lead one to hide beneath routine practices. Christ himself has blessed such an attempt: "Ask, and the gift will come; seek, and you shall find."

The famous saying of Pascal: "You would not seek me if you had not already found me", the expression of a burning faith, which so many psychologists have endorsed, was not in any way intended to oppose such a search. A man must seek to understand what he has already found; if he does not, he remains in darkness. Faith in God is not given as a learned answer to a riddle; when it is received, it seems supremely simple and familiar, even dazzlingly obvious, yet man must go through his human arguments and sternly set himself to the labour of the search, so as to deserve to learn that that faith was near him, was in him, and has guided his steps.

But is not Christ's praise of the spirit of little children a decisive argument against this "adult" faith, nourished by study and proof? No, for we must be careful not to misinterpret the text. Christ said: "He is greatest in the kingdom of heaven who will abase himself like this little child." This is not the same as if he had said, "This little child is the greatest in the kingdom of heaven." The accent is not directly on the spirit of childhood, but on the return to that spirit, a spirit essentially characterized by the word "little", that is, by the virtues of self-effacement and humility. We may recall his words about the flowers of the field, which neither toil nor spin, or about the "last who shall be first", and many others, all the profound sayings about the weak and the wretched and the oppressed. Childhood is not introduced as a particular age, but as the essential symbol of certain values.

So it is not in the name of some vague spirit of innocence that we shall, if we have to, defend the life of faith against the invasion of technology. The "good news" uses the language of reason. It knows the high value set on the existence of man, whom God has created and whose development he has willed—even if the end of that development is to be a return to the spirit of childhood. To speak to men, Christ waited until not only childhood had passed but also adolescence; and his disciples were all adults.

CHAPTER III

FALSE RECONCILIATIONS: SUPPRESSING THE PROBLEM

In trying to clarify the ideas concerning us here it may sometimes have seemed that an understanding has been taking shape in the background: could not technology, through which man ensures and declares his dominion over the material world, be simply a sort of direct extension of faith? May not that spirit of seeking and hoping for the Truth in confidence and joy which burns in faith find in technology a kind of sober and down-to-earth guarantee? We must not be deceived by such an illusion: faith, as I have said, is not merely a disposition of the mind, but has a content which is both vast and exact. It is still far too early to think of constructing or even of sketching out a true blending of the two. We must go on clearing the ground as honestly as we can, and first of all we must get out of the way a number of ideas which might prejudice the success of our inquiry.

There is a common opinion, among learned and unlearned alike, that technological progress is irreversible, that nothing can prevent man from ever more efficiently mastering and organizing the material world. Consequently a lot of good people, including a good many Christians, think that we are worrying over a problem that does not really exist. The solution is given before the problem is posed. The Christian faith must keep up with the times, and adapt itself to a situation which cannot possibly change. Let us accept Crazytown, since technology is triumphant and can only go on becoming more so; faith is mad to try to quarrel with it and to dish out in its indecision now praise, now blame, when its only proper task is to look for practical means of coming to terms with this overwhelming power. You take the earth and leave heaven to me.

There would be no point in a long discussion of such an oversimplified philosophy. Christianity has never been a kind of pragmatism. It has come to terms in the past, and will be able to come to terms in the future, with all sorts of political, social and economic régimes, but this does not mean that it has remained sublimely indifferent to them all. As soon as they appear to be overstepping the mark and becoming dangerous to man, they are challenged. The Church is afraid of no Attila or Napoleon or Hitler, nor will she turn aside to yield to the dictates of technology. The future life, of which she gives a sure hope and for which it is her task to prepare, rests on this present life, here and now.

But this excessive awe of the machine age, with its publicity and its noise, its bustle and its domestic comforts, is not the only attitude which can lead one to suppress—or to ask that we suppress—the idea of a possible conflict between the Christian faith and technology. If some men so far exaggerate the rôle of technology that the problem of life now becomes for them simply one of material organization, there are others who tend to forget technology altogether and happily bury their heads in the certitude of the Christian faith. Among these there are pessimists as well as optimists, sick men and strong, young people disillusioned before they have begun to live and philosophers led by long experience of life. They are not a strong group—even perhaps very weak, up against the "technicomanes"—but they deserve our consideration here. Their thought has, taken altogether, a rational structure, for even if they are obeying some sort of instinct, almost all of them seek to justify their attitude rationally. It is an odd thing that they are, perhaps, in their fanatical purity, the best supports of those who might seem to be their direct adversaries, those who cry, "Technology comes before faith" and "Technology is our life" and so on. In a sense, they offer these an alibi, for they provide these others with that reflective thinking, for use when needed, which they do not allow themselves the time to indulge in. For beyond any doubt, they play the part of men conquered by technology, and seem to have beaten the retreat; how can the others not consider themselves the victors?

Christians who are indifferent to the progress of technology, because they think their faith forbids their believing in it, and because they cling to the words of Christ: "And behold I am with you all through the days that are coming, until the consummation of the world", nevertheless play the same game as technology's wildest admirers. They do not want, indeed they positively refuse, to join in argument: nothing matters except what is eternal. If they hear that an essay subject has been set for schoolchildren, "The bicycle is more than a sport, it is a mark of human progress", they are not amused, even when they say that one thing gives way to another, that tomorrow the autocycle will replace the bicycle, and the day after, the autocycle will be replaced by the scooter, and so on—and none of it matters, the old iron, the grease, the pop-popping engine, the lot: the courts of the Lord are shut off from all this petty hullabaloo below.

While Thiers condemned the railway in the name of science and proved mathematically that tunnels would suffocate those who passed through them, a holy Curé d'Ars did not even guess that there were such problems. When a line was going to be constructed in his area, he never once put himself out to glance at the work, and died without ever having seen a train. Some agnostics, and even some Christians, come very close to ridiculing the Curé d'Ars as narrow-minded and reactionary. But we cannot agree with them. The holiness of the Curé d'Ars certainly has nothing to do with his contempt for railways, and this country priest was surely in any case one of the greatest of the saints, just as Flaubert is one of the great novelists, even if he could be reproached by Zola with having committed the mistake of never writing a novel about the rise of the machine.

It is difficult, when we think about it, to see what spiritual profit can be derived from this dangerous and unrealistic attitude. If sincere Christians, concerned with their Christian task, more or less ignore the existence of technology, there can be no objection in the name of Christianity, just as no one can, in the name of that same faith, rebuke a child who, despite hard work, gets low marks in science, or an intellectual who cannot change an electric light bulb without scorching the ends of his fingers. But may we not say that such an unrealistic attitude is to be condemned when reason and will are behind it?

In saying this, we are not criticizing the eremitical life. It is true that the hermit deliberately turns his back on the technological bustle of the modern world, but he does so for a higher Christian ideal which is not simply, for certain souls at least, a temptation to egoism. The eremitical life remains in theory one of the great forms of the religious life, and in very exceptional and well-tested cases the Church still sometimes authorizes one of her members to practise it. But in doing so, she does not take sides in a debate between the Christian faith and the modern world: she merely continues doing what she has done since the beginning, or nearly,

in admitting the possibility that a soul may deepen its faith
and piety through the eremitical life.

Christians who, without attacking technology directly or
ever becoming involved in such an attack, underestimate the
importance of material progress and the development of
modern organization, and set up strong water-tight bulk-
heads between such ideas and their faith in God and the
Church, have no lack of texts or arguments to defend their
attitude—supposing they would ever want to do so.

I was once present when two sisters quarrelled. One had
asked the other to watch the meat while it roasted. She had
just washed her hair, and sat in the sun in the kitchen reading
a novel. And the roast was burnt. "Aren't you ashamed
to be so lazy?" shouted the first. But the lazy one shrugged
her shoulders: "Didn't you know that a great saint once
asked God, 'Give me the grace to be useless'?" And can
we not see behind this everyday scene the shadows of
Martha and Mary, the contemporaries of Christ? "Martha,
Martha, how many cares and troubles thou hast! But only
one thing is necessary; and Mary has chosen for herself the
best part of all, that which shall never be taken away from
her." How many times has one heard this quoted, so very re-
proachfully, as if to say: "Poor little twentieth-century man,
with your great furnaces and your reactors and your washing
machines, you cut such a fine figure before the Almighty!
Put an end to this farce, put out your fires, and pray!"

And there is another passage, no less well known, which
eloquently supports this:

> See how the wild lilies grow; they do not toil or spin; and
> yet I tell you that even Solomon in all his glory was not arrayed
> like one of these. If God, then, so clothes the grasses of the
> field, which today live and will feed the oven tomorrow, will
> he not be much more ready to clothe you, men of little faith?
> Do not fret, then, asking, What are we to eat? or What are we
> to drink? or How shall we find clothing? It is for the heathen

to busy themselves over such things; you have a Father in heaven who knows that you need them all. Make it your first care to find the kingdom of God, and his approval, and all these things shall be yours without the asking.

Too many Christians interpret the words of the New Testament as though they had a moral like one of Aesop's fables, applicable in some detail in the visible world about them. But they are primarily general teachings on a very high level, and their meaning, which is fixed by the Church, is not always evident at first sight. In any case, the Christian knows beyond all question that Gospel texts never contradict one another. Or, if we prefer to use the expressions of those who oppose the unity of the Gospel teaching, let us say that there are not many moralities in the Gospel, but only one. Hence we cannot find any praise of discomfort, or of unpreparedness, or of destitution, in the two texts quoted; if we do, we shall find them opposed by a good many others, which clearly support the need for technology.

In a prayer which God himself has given us we ask him to "give us our daily bread". This implies that even materially we are always in God's hands, and also that in order to make sure of our daily bread, made from grain harvested only once a year, we men must face and resolve as far as we can the many problems of preserving grain and marketing it and so on.

Like Christ, who was a carpenter, and like the apostles, who were fishermen or tax-gatherers, men must work, if only to provide their families' livelihood. "If any one of yourselves is asked by his son for bread, will he give him a stone?" But how can a man satisfy his son if he does not work, if he does not earn some of those pieces of money, in no way to be condemned in themselves, bearing the likeness of Caesar's head, some of those silver coins which a woman seeks so carefully and rightly when she has lost one

—"does she not light a lamp, and sweep the house, and search carefully until she finds it?"

What of the miracle of the multiplication of the loaves? It is a miracle of organization, of order, of distribution: by his divine power, Christ multiplies the resources of human technology, but first he uses them. The miracle at Cana, expressly called the first miracle of Jesus, is perhaps even more typical, for here the generosity of God is seen even more clearly. Here, God provides man not with what is indispensable, nor even with what is necessary, but something over and above his needs. Those invited to the wedding had already quenched their thirst, and the miracle was done to "make known the glory that was his".

It is a miracle to delight the heart of Breughel. The principle strikes upon the vision like lightning: God passes and acts, using the laws of nature as and when he wishes, without ever having to take the slightest account of men. Yet this does not prevent God from respecting that which he can surpass. In the field of domestic economy, the miracle at Cana hallows the making good of a fault of the human organizers, who had been somewhat skimpy. Refreshments have to be worked out, just as do surfaces and volumes, and even if this aspect of things does not occur to abstract theorists who immediately think of industry when they think of technology (wrongly), the miracle at Cana goes still further. It justifies, with marvellous brevity, the great ambition of material progress, which is to increase man's well-being. Without revealing to anyone the secrets of the transmutation he works, by which water is changed into good wine, Christ clearly recognizes man's right to seek to master matter in order to satisfy his reasonable desires.

These examples, to which many more could be added, are enough to show how we should read the text about the lilies of the field. No phrase in that text suggests that we should be altogether indifferent to the material aspects of life; that would be both impossible for human nature and contrary to reason. All that is necessary, and it is absolutely necessary, is that those aspects should not so fill a man's mind that he is oblivious to those aspects which have regard to God, which are the higher. This is not a matter of arranging the timetable properly, of how one uses one's time, but, as always, a matter of the spirit. Martha would bring no reproach on herself if she used her vacuum cleaner or cleaned her windows, and sang or prayed as she did so, and never got cross with those who did their housework less well than she did. There is always room for our Lady's tumbler; and there is room today for the girl at the work-bench or the spinning machine or the telephone, who tries to like her job and her "little world"—and who is thus, without thinking about it, very close to her God.

It is difficult to accept that the Christian faith can allow technology to go on being so wretchedly short-sighted. Christ has given us his example. The Christian faith is in principle capable of taking up every problem, and far from the words of Christ—"I shall be with you till the consummation of the world"—entitling the Christian to withdraw from others and smother himself in a dismal and lukewarm religion, they encourage him to face up to his own times.

CHAPTER IV

FALSE RECONCILIATIONS:

GOD AS WATCHMAKER

If the Church must know the world whose salvation is her responsibility, and if it is therefore impossible for Christians to avoid becoming involved with technology, it presumably follows that genuine cooperation is desirable.

Not so very long ago, such cooperation would have been difficult. The phrase "inferiority complex" is often abused, but it might properly be applied to Christianity fifty or sixty years ago. Science was in the ascendant, and seemed to possess the keys of life. Scientists were going, it seemed, to solve all man's problems, mystery was an outmoded, medieval idea, and God could be relegated to Folk Museums. If there were Christians among the scientists, the fact was kept quietly in the background, as if a religious faith was a sort of shameful disease.

But things are no longer so. Such over-confidence in science is out of fashion. There have been two terrible wars. With or without the scientists' consent and will, research scientists in the great powers have striven and laboured to produce ever more effective, that is, more murderous weapons, providing governments and their armed forces with the means of killing men in their tens of millions, and substituting for international peace a strange state of tension, a balance of terror.

But the scientists' present modesty is not entirely due to a feeling of remorse. The more science has advanced, the more scientists have become aware of the darkness beyond, of the room and the need for something else, something more, a philosophy or a religion. Not that the majority of scientists, even in Christian countries, subscribe to some religious faith; there are still militant atheists among them, but there are certainly more who practise some religion. The hypotheses of science, such as that of the expanding universe, no longer seem to anyone to constitute objections to transcendence. There is room now for "peaceful coexistence" between science and religion.

Yet in practice, the lower down the scale one moves, from those who create techniques to those who teach them, and from those who instruct to those who use them, the more one finds the old pride and confidence in science and technology. The old over-confidence is out of fashion, I said. So it is; but it has left its legacy, and outside the circle of educated scientists, where it is hardly now to be found, it finds strong echoes in the mass of ordinary people.

Yet although such people do not realize that religious faith is not wholly strange to them, that it lies waiting in their own innermost being, it would be quite useless to try to influence them by argument. They cannot yet be touched by the most cogent reasoning, however well constructed by philosophers: "Eyes have they, but see not." Men must first know how to apprehend God in what cannot be seen before they can apprehend him in what can.

When the Christian faith approaches technology, it must abandon the grand ideas of the order of the universe, of God as a super-watchmaker. The temptation to use these ideas is very great, for technology relies, in its exploitation of the world, on the laws of its architecture; but that would be to fall into a trap.

The scientific and always rational complications of man-made machinery and apparatus symbolize for the Christian the obedience of matter to the planning of a higher being, but it would be foolish unthinkingly to expect the same reaction from a non-believer. Listen to the words of Mr Fadeyev on Moscow radio in 1958: "Church-folk assert that the world beyond and its spiritual inhabitants are incorporeal and immaterial, and therefore cannot be seen or sensed by human beings. But these human beings construct rockets and satellites and instruments to study phenomena which our sense organs cannot perceive—storms and X-rays from the sun and magnetic fields and so on. If these supernatural beings really existed, science would long ago have detected their existence with its powerful methods of research." More recently, in 1962, the second Soviet cosmonaut, Titov, far from producing an up-to-date "The heavens declare the glory of God", only said as he stepped out of his space capsule: "I met no one out there and could have met no one." There was, after all, no air. While he was in orbit, he received signals from a Japanese radio station broadcasting in Russian, talking of God and his saints. The cosmonaut smiled at the memory: "I should have liked to send a message to that station," he said, "but I thought: what's the use? They might think that God is speaking to them."

The scientific order on which all technology rests, from the most complicated electronic brain to a boy scout's knife, is not the same as the religious order. It is important to be clear about this, because any alliance between technology and faith which was based on deceit or confusion or half-truths would not last a moment.

Everyone knows the great principle of the conservation of matter, which was established by Lavoisier. Its obvious truth strikes the mind immediately, and no one is surprised that Pasteur, who was a scientist and a Christian, derived from its application some of his most famous discoveries. Should one not rather be astonished that mankind had to wait for the eighteenth century to express a truth so simple and so obvious? How easy to lay the blame for this tardiness on the back of the Church! But what ought to be said is that this principle, which seems indisputable and indubitable, and the applications of which are evident in all our daily lives, has not perhaps that firmness, that ability to stand any test, with which we credit it.

A man learns to drive a car, a common enough process nowadays. His teachers and instructors and manuals of instruction all tell him that engine failure or any other sort of breakdown must have a good material cause, and is not due to anything odd or strange; the cause may be difficult to discover, but it is there, it can be exactly and certainly known and the careful and conscientious driver will make it a point of honour to diagnose it for himself.

A girl studies child care. Whether she does it in a special class or in a welfare centre, she will hear a good deal said about the importance to the baby of good and regular feeding. All that she hears about this will rest firmly and faithfully on Lavoisier's principle. You measure the amount of milk, you weigh the baby: it is as if you are dealing with a small plant.

Think of all those childish games which the press, radio and especially television offer to the so-called adults of the world, to test their intelligence or their culture or their education. With a terrible efficiency they assist in fixing firmly in men's minds just those commonplace assumptions which brought them into being in the first place: there is nothing unknown, everything can be numbered, everything is explained in the pocket-book. Consider with what patient labour a house-painter committed to memory the names of

all the papal encyclicals, without exception, or an old lady
the genealogies of all the tailors who ever dressed Mozart,
or an Eskimo teacher the signs of the European inns of the
year 1731!

In the world outside as much as in the depths of consciousness the principle of the simplicity of the world finds plenty
of matter for convincing propaganda. All the typical
monuments of man striving ever more obviously to declare
his power: sky-scrapers and factories in the towns and
suburbs, dams and petrol refineries and aerodromes in the
deserts—all tending to have the same functional simplicity
of line. Surely there have never been raised on the earth's
surface so many sprawling cities or such piles of waste matter;
never have the masses of material described as buildings
been less assured of the future approval of their builders, or
more likely to be replaced by others, or even by a reeking
crater. Yet despite this there are and will be now almost
everywhere those shapes and masses and concrete tracks to
show that man has the keys to the universe, and that they
are big and simple keys.

It is true that the complexity of the control panels of a
modern aeroplane or the inside of a wireless station are less
reassuring images, but the layman very quickly leaves it to
the experts to cope easily and happily with all those buttons
and wires. It is after all, he reflects, only a matter of training
and of memory. And if, exceptionally, the game gets too
complicated for the human mind, some friendly robot will
finds its way about without difficulty. Rather than this
making an approach by religion possible, such an attitude
logically suggests a professional warping of nature. Technology continually displays the value of inductive reasoning,
and there is a danger that it may lead the mind to use it all
the time. Exactly known causes always produce their regular
consequences. It is clear, proper, convenient; nothing is
lost, nothing is created; if there are two ways out, everything

which does not use the first must use the second, and if you
can say, "Paul is eating an apple", then you can also say,
"An apple is being eaten by Paul", *Q.E.D.*

All very convincing: but God the watchmaker is not
enough for religious faith. The God who makes himself
known in secret, by personal and ineffable signs, to each
single soul, cannot be this First Workman in the World,
this Supreme Artificer who loves a "good piece of work"
that can be taken to pieces and put together again at will.
We have become very familiar through theology with an
idea which satisfies our reasons and our hearts, that of the
divine plan. And how could we doubt that the Creator of
Genesis intended to give a meaning to his work? But the
God of that divine plan and of Genesis is not God the watchmaker, the God of machinery with no mystery. The short
sentence, "My kingdom is not of this world", is universal in
its application, and we can understand it also of the realm
of the intelligence, where the divine plan—or at least as
much as we can begin to understand—shows itself to be
strangely confusing for our strict logic. The God of the
divine plan is the God of the workers called at the eleventh
hour, the God of grace and of the thunder-cloud. If the
cosmonaut Titov did not meet him in the empty spaces of
the sky where, in his boasting impudence, he located such a
meeting-place, still less can we expect to meet him in our
daily lives if we reduce his rôle to that of a super-mechanic,
the inventor and builder of our fine modern society, of one
of those factories which seems to be a sort of glass-
house.

Just as slogans such as "Strength through joy" and
"Education through play" and "French without tears"
have been laughed out of court, so we must banish the ideas
of "God through mechanics" and "God through things"
and so on, which some have offered modern minds, rushing
on too fast, as a sort of sugary pill to be swallowed.

"God the watchmaker" is very wide of the mark. A Portuguese saying, which one is glad to see quoted increasingly in such discussions as this, warns us: "God writes straight on crooked lines." That is, technology, with its straight-line reasoning and its neatly worked-out equations, finds it much more difficult to discover him in the perpetually changing continuum of our existence than does a good will open to mystery; in other words, the Creator is better revealed to the artist and the poet than to the engineer or the administrator or the comfort-conscious housewife, at least so far as these latter are unwilling to step beyond their professions and their routine work to think about the world.

The world which meets the eyes of man is no longer the earthly paradise, nor is man in his original perfect state of innocence when he looks at it. So all his contemplation and reflection must, it seems, end sooner or later in recognizing in the reality that surrounds him defects and monsters and useless organs; he must be roused to anger by the many mistakes and faults which strike his eye when he looks at life; he may even beat his head desperately against the absurdities and the riddles of this mess, this jumbled din, this waste of life, this pointlessness.

Can we praise God in the perfection of a leaf, the beauty of a bird's song, or the delicate shades of a lichen? Of course we can, and we can altogether agree with Gide when he says: "There is a great joy in simply saying: the fruit of the palm is called a date, and it is a delicious fruit." But a watchmaker or a mechanic or a statistician who sang the praises of the world for the number and the intricacy of its wheels, obvious proofs of a divine goodness in its planning, would surely be brutally interrupted by other watchmakers and mechanics and statisticians who would accuse him of skipping over the important problems of evil and suffering. It would be dishonest and vain to pretend to oneself that these problems, which can be faced by the Christian armed by his faith, did not constitute for all men—even for Christians at some time in their lives—a serious cause of internal doubts and debate. Quite probably those who are not so learned or intellectual put these problems in very simple terms, which may make a philosopher smile; but they too live as much as the philosopher, and have as much right to speak.

To all those high-minded people, more Christian than Christ or the pope, who hold that moral resignation to evil and suffering is only a dodge, Christ himself gave a great lesson in humility, when he raised from the dead his friend Lazarus, or Jairus' daughter, or the widow's son at Naim. Think of this last example: Jesus was walking along a road and met, just outside the town, a funeral procession. They told him they were going to bury the only son of a widow; and she was there, her face ravaged with grief. Jesus was moved with pity for her: he is the consoler, neither wondering at nor irritated by tears. Performed for this mother, afflicted as only too many are, this miracle, like the others for Jairus and for the sisters of Lazarus, cannot be seen as an exceptional and unfair favour. It is a recognition that even in God's eyes there can be, in one of the ordinary sufferings of man, an element of scandal and injustice. A reaction against this is inevitable; but it certainly exists, and it is sometimes overwhelming and calls for forbearance.

If some people plunged in misery revolt against God because others selfishly enjoy great material blessings, or if millions of men feel like revolting against him because they need an outlet for their fear of an atomic war, God suffers because of it, but he understands—and the Church also understands.

If technology can help men move towards the faith, it is not because of or by means of its intellectual methods, its simple and direct logic, however successful these may appear. Endlessly the world moves towards order, and

endlessly it draws away from it. When a Christian speaks of
war and famine and injustice, does he not leave out what is
most grievous, if not most serious, when he forgets to be
quite accurate? For not the least of the causes of the scandal
felt in the mind of the technologist when he observes the
world "as it is", is the spectacle offered to his view by so
many "official" Christians. We must, it is true, be careful
not to exaggerate, and must remember how wickedly (in the
satanic sense of the word) relentless the mind of man is in
suspecting believers of hypocrisy. But with all our care we
cannot long put off the conclusion: those who are known
as Christians, taken all together, do not sufficiently practise
the virtues they preach. This is not our personal opinion
only: we are but repeating what we have so often read or
heard on so many different occasions from authorized
sources, in sermons, or pastoral letters or religious books.
The majority of Christians are seen to be just as greedy,
selfish, proud, impure and cruel as others who are not
Christian. Their religion seems to be only a façade, and
certainly there are a good many agnostics who live more
Christian lives than they do.

Certainly we have been warned, in the Gospel: "Not
everyone who says, Lord, Lord . . ."; and the marvellous
company of the saints should prevent anyone from falling
into bitterness and despair. But this is not to deny the fact,
paradoxical and grievous for the strong in faith themselves,
and capable of terribly depressing and worrying the great
crowd of weaker brethren.

Compared with the fine productions, clean and neat and
new, of technology, the world is too often like an old
checker-board which has been jogged so that the pieces are
no longer in their places, but lie over the lines between the
white and black squares. To get back from the disorder
and the contradictions and the cruelty to the original fresh-
ness of his lost paradise, to find the pure swiftness of the

spring in the fens and bogs of the world, man can hardly rely on technological reasoning. Technology has not been given the words that are necessary to cure at their root man's troubles and his anxiety. All the pleasure and the well-being which is produced by technology leaves the essential questions untouched.

CHAPTER V

ANTAGONISM

The position I have tried to take up is by no means anti-technological. I am not trying to belittle technology in its own sphere, but only to ask it to stay there, knowing that that sphere is very large. So long as it keeps to its own field, so long as it no longer tries to substitute its own values for those of the Christian faith and to become almost a sort of religion of material research with the earthly salvation of man as its goal, technology can render religion many eminent services.

But to come to a satisfactory end of our dialectical difficulties, all Christians must agree to resolve the problem by an honourable agreement which categorically and unambiguously safeguards the primacy of the spirit.

We have mentioned those who would reduce the relations between technology and religion to the sort of living together and yet not together that is typical of some suburban societies, where each lives close to others and no one knows anyone else. But this will not do when it comes to ideas: sooner or later, they meet. When they do, they must question each other, observe each other, study each other: and then become either allies or enemies. Almost all those Christians whose first object is to avoid having to mix with technology eventually have to give up such an intention. Some of them, reluctantly but sincerely, try to examine and understand technology so as to make it serve their faith. Almost all the rest become the fanatical enemies of technology.

These too must be heard, though we cannot ourselves agree with them. Among them, all sincere Christians, are philosophers and writers and good priests, thinking men of great experience who know how to turn a striking phrase. Very few people can say that they have not at some time or another been close to supporting their opinions. It is surely possible to belong partly to both camps: how many Englishmen find themselves part Conservative, part Labour? And how many Americans are both Republicans and Democrats? So it is not so paradoxical that a Christian thinking about his religion may hide within himself, almost all the time, both a friend and an enemy of technology. Almost continually, of course, he is making a choice; but, again almost continually, he refrains from rejecting absolutely and violently and finally the alternative he has not chosen. Even if we think that those Christians who are professed enemies of technology are fanatically and desperately fighting for a lost cause, they surely deserve our respect. Almost all that they say—and they say it, no doubt, too dogmatically and too cantankerously—needs to be said. Thanks to them, Christians are provided with the materials for an argument which each must carry on within himself as part of the collective drama of man.

They proceed by scientifically analysing the religious phenomenon; they dissect modern man and the modern world. They frequently come very close to Manicheism, and give the impression of over-estimating, without being over-explicit about it, the part played by demoniac spirits, whose presence they detect in countless objects, societies, habits and so on, in a sort of pandiabolism. But they reject any suspicion of heresy and, except when they are carried away by the argument, assert that they are only attacking abuses, wrong states of mind.

To try to understand what they do calmly and objectively, I shall attempt to keep the argument clear of passions and emotions; but I am aware before beginning that this is really what is called a pious hope. For at this point in the argument technology is seen in all its breadth and scope, under all its aspects, both as an enormous mass of material equipment and also as a vast dream of man's; the case for or against it in the name of Christianity becomes part of the heated and ever renewed battle between those who believe moral progress to be possible and those who refuse to believe it.

It is a strange battle, in which the division is no longer between professing Christians and non-Christians, but between two basic attitudes to the world around us, which according to one side, crushes us, and according to the other, sets us free. There are Christians in both camps, good and active Christians who take sides deliberately in a practical and ecumenical spirit which it is good to see. In the fashionable phrase of the day, every human being feels himself "involved", or "committed". There is no *a priori* method of guessing to which group this or that person belongs; but, as the saying goes, God will recognize his own, and we must always remember that people are changing sides almost the whole time.

Gabriel Marcel has joined in accusing technology of degrading man: he refers to all those methods of achieving comfort and material control over the world which have been so suddenly made available to man, and are now his without demanding from him any real mental effort. What is wrong is not that we have hot and cold taps in the bathroom, but that we take them for granted, as the natural privilege of twentieth-century man, his inalienable advantage over his fellow man who dwelt in caves, and over the animals.

It is a relentless circle: to begin with, the philosopher recognizes that some kinds of technology can be healthy enough; it all depends on how a man uses them. But there's the rub: the sort of technological thought which inspires the modern world, and which has as its purpose to simplify once and for all the tasks that men have to do, is so dominated by concern for material efficiency that it cannot but do all it can to simplify man too as much as possible and to free him from personal thinking, now looked on as a burden. Faster! Faster! Without bothering to look back at the fruitful and difficult business of its invention, the user of any given technology confines himself to seeing what movements he has to make, which more and more have to imitate those of a machine. Fifty years ago it used to be said that rough industrial work had made a large number of individuals into "the proletariat". Today our "press-button" society reifies—"thingifies"—man: it uses him at different levels like a characterless wheel, of "standard" quality, completely interchangeable, and is utterly unconcerned with the particular richness of each.

Psychologists have said, and are always saying, that technology takes the place of man in doing "inferior" tasks, and leaves him free for higher thought. A good deal of the time now taken up with such earthly considerations as the struggle against hunger or cold could now, thanks to domestic appliances, to automation, to audio-visual methods of instruction, and so on, be given to leisure, to art, to general culture, to scientific or philosophical research. So there is nothing in principle harmful about living in a "press-button" civilization. Mankind must think, above all, in terms of the future. We have now summed up and established firmly all the results of man's past thought and labour in the material equipment now at the world's disposal; that must now be used as a springboard for a new, and even more rapid, leap forward.

Such an argument, the psychological basis of which he rejects, is accused of naïvety by Marcel. According to him, human nature is always the same, and it would be futile to expect that it was going to become nobler and higher and purer as man's power over the physical world increased. On the contrary, we must be extremely careful. The proliferation of material goods, of consumer goods or of capital assets, is a threat to the spirit and the mind. Even though the progress of medicine and surgery have increased the average expectation of life, and even though legislation has sensibly reduced the hours a man works, the economic and social climate in the nations called "advanced" has become so oppressive that the time available for spiritual reflection has grown continually less and less, and less and less worth having. Man's consciousness is filled with the tangible, the visible, the material.

Whatever happens in this argument, the Christian must be happy to see that all men, as individuals or in groups, take part in this debate about progress; for because of the ideas it involves it is, whether the materialists want it to be or not, a religious debate, one which could hasten the coming of the Kingdom. However technology is to be judged, it offers this advantage to religion, that for the present at any rate it obliges men to consider, all the time, what is the meaning of their presence on earth, and also, beyond the problems of material survival, to worry about their whole future.

It is the present and future lot of the whole of mankind which has concerned such writers as Duhamel, Huxley, Valéry, Alain—none of them egocentrics, jealous for the security of their ivory towers. Though they are full of admiration for the intellectual effort behind the achievements of technology, they fear its unnecessarily feverish haste, its mad need to do something, to make changes, which makes its patronage dangerous for man: under the pretext of making more sure of each man's essential physical nourishment and well-being, it is perhaps shamelessly casting on to the scrap-heap the beauties of the world and of art, which are also essential needs of man. Not only would Gandhi have sympathized with such fears, but Einstein in his later years was so afraid at having discovered a sort of fundamental weakness in technology—did it not serve good and evil quite indifferently?—that he is said to have joked that, if he could have had his time over again, he would have left science alone and sold papers or cleaned boots. Nor is such an idea simply to be put down to old age: you cannot explain away such despair by talking of cholesterol or the hardening of the arteries. Einstein had fled to the "free world" from Hitler's Germany, and devoted himself to its service to assist the victory of the Spirit: how could he shut his eyes to the horrors that at the last moment accompanied that victory?

The old enthusiasm for science and technological progress has gone, and the sickness of modern youth is a sort of worried irritation: *ennui*—the word is used by Bernanos' country priest to sum up the spirit of his parish. His villagers were worried and annoyed because they felt they were less modern, less crowded, and thereby less alive than those who live in the big cities. They were jealous of the noise and the bustle and the lights, the swarming mass of men and cars, the rows of streets and great buildings. Poor country cousins! All the great film comics, such as Charlie Chaplin and Jacques Tati, have found this same *ennui* at the very heart of modernism and its noisy and stereotyped delights. In *Monsieur Hulot's Holiday*, there was an image at once amusing and tragic: that of the playful waves on the little beach, deserted by the holidaymakers for their midday meal in the hotel—one could hear the sea alternately laughing and crying: God filled it with beauty, but *they* have eyes and they see not.

Yet when we examine it and think about it, we can discern under the wild admiration which some profess for technology either a deep but pretentious naïvety like that of a twentieth-century Monsieur Jourdain—"So people of quality believe in technology?" "Of course!" "They do? Then I shall have to myself"—or a cover for business speculations. The human being, the man, described by Horace or Boileau or La Bruyère, is still alive in these businessmen, these executives, whose names call up the greatest enterprises that have changed the world, but who about themselves want quiet and solitude and big trees. Someone wants them on the telephone, but they are "in conference"—fishing; when a journalist asked him about his own tastes, Le Corbusier sang the praises of a hedgerow or a mature Camembert or a glass of good red wine; Eisenhower was generalissimo of a vast army, and became the president of the most powerful nation on earth, but the image that probably lives most vividly in people's minds is that of a man playing golf.

This being said, it is too late to try to stop Christianity from recognizing its obligation to technology, and establishing perfectly friendly relations with it; just as it would be a waste of time to emphasize the fact that this relationship pertains to very special fields. Beneath the surface, the unity of technological thought makes game of frontiers. Whoever draws on one kind of technology loses any right, not to criticize other kinds, but to challenge the principles of technology themselves. And Christianity is in just that position. It has asked for the precise and detailed help of several techniques, from which it has demanded more than simply material aid, more or less extensive but always limited (such as the installation of loudspeakers in church, or of microphones for the Second Vatican Council): it has asked for a real cooperation for the more effective accomplishment of its task.

Twentieth-century Christians owe a great debt to modern exegesis, which has made so much easier the approach to the essential texts of Revelation. A great many papal encyclicals pay tribute to the methods of that exegesis and to the

number and the value of its results. Now that exegesis, guided
by the Holy Spirit, basically depends on the various techniques used in dealing with the problems of the decipher-
ment of ancient texts, using the methods of linguistics,
history, sociology and so on. In the end, of course, our
knowledge of Revelation infinitely surpasses all such supports; yet we can still say that at a given time in its formation that knowledge was accompanied and helped and
strengthened by technology.

The sustained interest shown by the Church, for the
accomplishment of her own mission, in contemporary
sociology and psychology, moreover, is only a particular
case, a modern example, of a general readiness to accept the
activities of men. It was not the experts, the technicians, that
Christ chased out of the Temple, but the insolent and the
hypocrites. How were the money-changers and the sellers of
doves more "expert" than the fisherman Peter and the tax-
collector Matthew? And there is a deep meaning in the
picture of the good shepherd, the man who "knows his
sheep", who is not merely vaguely interested in them, but
counts them, knows their habits, watches over them and
cares for them. He is *the* likeness of Christ. But he is also the
model for mankind learning to know and develop his
resources for the good of all. The parable of the talents
teaches the same lesson.

Nor has the Church ever, as such, favoured obscurantism
or stagnation, or opposed material progress in itself. In the
Middle Ages, country clergy taught the peasants how to
clear the land of trees and rocks and how to sow their crops,
while in the towns they assisted the city corporations in their
guilds. "When Adam delved and Eve span, where was then
the gentleman?" To this rhyme another saying may be
added: "When the bishop of the Sahara journeys by air
several times a week, and when Pius XII followed revolu-
tionary medical developments, or John XXIII addressed the

pilgrims to a Eucharistic Congress by radio, when Paul VI is crowned in St Peter's Square before an audience of many millions thanks to television, where are the enemies of science and technology?"

Fair enough, perhaps; and even if this is only on the fringe of the problem, we clearly cannot entirely adopt as our own the criticisms of technology so cleverly constructed by Marcel. A human being is not simply a mysterious instant in the earth's history, with no depth: at a particular point of time and place he is born, he becomes incarnate in physical reality, in the continuum of physical existence, and moves inevitably towards death. When he grows up, he finds he has to accept a lot of responsibilities, and that there is no point in arguing about it: he has to live, to accept and to take up his life, and his confraternity with countless other men.

This being so, according to what principle can we ban technology? It is the creation of man's intelligence; it can and must join with the virtue of hope to sustain man, body and soul, in his difficult task of living, for through the first it helps the second—"For the spiritual is itself carnal." Péguy so succinctly expressed this truth in this line that he has been credited with its discovery, though St Thomas Aquinas and many others had said the same before.

Can there be a good and bad technology, in the sense that there are good and bad films? The situation is much less clear. We have no justification for vilifying technology as such. It constitutes a perpetual storehouse for man's use, and simply because we know it contains some bad things, we should not forget that it also contains a lot of good. If we do, we allow demoniac spirits a power in this world they do not really possess; which is what happened to Bernanos, despite his genius.

Christianity must take up, initially, a favourable attitude to technology, even if it must inevitably examine it carefully when the necessity arises, in all its applications, and is bound to criticize its excesses, its errors and its omissions. So the Christian may reasonably admit that a great part of the philosopher's criticisms, in his analysis of our society now, seems to be justified. The idea of the separateness, of the sundering from the world, of the Christian has nowadays become highly significant, with the development of technology. The gap is, alas!, widening between our blazing optimism and a reality which all too often is debased. We must hold to our hope and stand fast in the fight. The Christian is more and more like an army surgeon operating while the battle rages about him: he must stay at his post, and think only of the wounded being brought in, without allowing any thoughts of faint-heartedness or tiredness to interrupt his humble work for the suffering flesh of man, in his defence of the frontiers of a kingdom of peace and gentleness.

This argument must not be pressed too far. It would be too easy, even without incurring the reproach of being a *laudator temporis acti*, to pick out at random a thousand pitiable or horrible details of our technological civilization, a thousand pretentious or ridiculous aspects of contemporary behaviour, many of which might lead us to wonder whether the very idea of material progress is not somewhat spurious, and more and more deserving of attack: the great increase in the numbers suffering from nervous diseases, both young and old, in the "highly civilized" nations; the congestion and air pollution in the great cities, the symbols of the constructive genius of the age; the noise, and the terrible waste—it is said in Canada that the waste of an American city could feed a European one, and that from a European city could feed one in Asia; the return to practices of torture by so-called Christian nations; the excessive luxury; the universal malaise of adolescence—beatniks, delinquents and so on; the increase in crime and in suicides; the barbaric desecration of the beauty of nature and the

lonely places; and so on and on—we could go on giving
example after example.

What is more depressing than a journey in the late
evening through the residential area of a large city? Scarcely
a pedestrian to be seen, except perhaps some shivering chap
exercising his dog, while in all the houses people sleep
or watch television: they have had enough of driving and
stopping and starting during the day. In this grim-visaged
atmosphere, in which pleasure is really distraction, and in
which distraction takes the form of a public service, carefully
timed, commercialized, "big business"—we can hardly say
that the life of the spirit is benefiting from it or that
Christianity is encouraged to spread.

Besides this, Church leaders have energetically protested
against the sanctimonious methods used by the commercial
world to debase for its own profit the great feasts of Chris-
tendom. Poor Christmas, worked on and analysed and taken
over by the business brains, so that from its true nature of a
recall to humility they have passed cunningly and deftly to a
vast invitation to spend more, to indulge in all kinds of
extravagances at home and socially, to give rein to all forms
of weakness and vanity. Christmas, for hundreds of millions
of people, is no longer Bethlehem or the fulfilment of the
prophecies, nor the Incarnation of Christ, but the great
season of the business "boom", of big orders, when the
confectioners no longer need to compete. Think of it:
Christmas comes sufficiently long after the summer holidays,
which may have upset people's budgets, and when it is
over, it is the season for winter sports, so that the great
organizers of the bazaar can go off and enjoy the relaxation
they have earned.

It would help if one could say that it is only a time of
transition: but the forces of materialism are advancing
everywhere, and show no sign that they ever intend retreat-
ing.

After the passage, in 1936, of some great social legislation in France, legislation deeply Christian in its spirit of justice, an ex-President of the Council thought fit to speak out against what he called "the sordid materialism of the lower classes"; he was rich and fond of his own comforts and he is now dead, God rest his soul. But surely it was an incredibly stupid and offensive thing to say! All the same, even if it is wrong to restrict the taunt of materialism to one section of society, and if the idea of materialism is itself somewhat ambiguous, since matter also is from God, and we cannot condemn it in principle without falling into Manicheism, it must be said that the behaviour of those today called Christians betrays a certain feverishness, under the influence of advancing techniques, and a spread of materialist tendencies which is altogether to be condemned.

There could be a materialism which was healthy and moderate and circumscribed, which would restrain a certain hazy idealism which tends to wander too widely, by firmly and discreetly opposing to it the true rôle and the true value of matter. There was a time when spiritual thinkers thought themselves not merely entitled but even bound by their doctrines to deny the reality of the physical world. There is still a tendency to do this, which Christianity must resist. But unfortunately technology is very far, in its materialism, from halting at a stage that right reason would think proper; its excitement is unbridled, and every minute, every second, it expands and bursts its bounds.

Between those nations which accept historical materialism as their foundation, and those which push ahead the claims of industrial development, of productivity, and of the intensive exploitation of all sources of energy, there has arisen an involuntary and very significant understanding: both talk loudly and long about greatness and wealth and the primacy of material problems. Frequently, of course, the big businessmen of the "western" countries also mention

God and man, and we cannot simply dismiss this as hypocrisy. Only it is very rare that the speeches in which these mentions occur are buttressed by any true defence of the Spirit. Force and material power are much more often heard praised in their sentences.

I ought not to have been surprised to receive, among all the technico-religious-commercial stuff, a letter about the first communion of a son, which began with a reference to St Luke in Gothic lettering: "Verily, verily, I say unto you, whoever does not receive this as a little child. . . ." It was a large piece of glossy paper, with the heading of a firm of watchmakers. I wondered what was coming: "Sir or Madam, It is close now, this day of days which your dear, small child is waiting for. . . ." And then, suddenly, the thought switched round a hundred and eighty degrees. The religious aspect had been briefly sketched in: now to business— "What expense to anticipate: meals, presents, dress! This company has worked out very carefully a special programme which will enable you to balance your budget."

We can imagine the anger Léon Bloy would have felt had he opened such a letter, and the oath he would have dropped at that charming quotation from St Luke. But the sad thing is that of the tens of thousands of mothers and fathers who read those words, the great majority, as we know, though of course from only a restricted circle, evinced no reaction at all. Unless they could find time to think about it, they could see no scandal in it. Yet is not this base hypocrisy the same sort of thing as the commercialism that surrounds the great sanctuaries and exploits and degrades the faith at Lourdes or Lisieux? It is an ancient evil: some of the early Fathers warn pilgrims of the dangers of Jerusalem. But the technique has improved.

Perhaps my readers will jib at these references to behaviour which, in practice, they accept—even if they secretly deplore it—and will decide that I am exaggerating the responsibilities of technology. It may seem that whenever we are faced with any of the evils of our contemporary world, we persist in protesting, "Ah! Technology again!"

Now this is true. We are only resigning ourselves to an attitude which seems inevitable. Nineteenth and twentieth century man, forcing the pace of an evolution contained in germ in the nature of the most primitive man, has now introduced technology and techniques into every corner of the globe as into every corner of the world of thought; and, far from slowing down, the process is increasing in pace all the time. It must be said that man's activity, man's control, is never quite done away with in the process: when there is something wrong, it is he who is to be blamed, he the living creature made in God's image, not some chemical substance or brute machine, or a too complicated and extensive programme of organization. But to acquit technology on the level of morality, which can only pertain to persons, does not solve the whole problem. There is left the vast field of material responsibilities, and there we immediately come up against technology. Inspired by individual men, it has now gone beyond them and increased its importance in an unprecedented way, and now places extraordinary resources at the disposition of vice. Trickery and deception, first, and idleness. Suppose a man wants to avoid the responsibility for some fault: he has only to apply to technology, to look through its card index, and there he will easily find a material cause ready-made for his fault. The world is now swarming with excuses and motives, precedents and guarantees and explanations provided by the countless multitude of things produced by technology, or by those vast collections of men made possible by technology, or by the mysteries attaching to its marvels. This man has committed murder? No: this man hasn't—his hand merely made certain motions within a vast system of causes and effects. The mental troubles of the age committed murder;

the constant flow of crime films committed murder; fear of
nuclear war committed murder; the mental disturbances
caused by living fourteen stories up committed murder; and
so on. In the same way a road hog is said not to be responsible because he was driving under the influence of alcohol;
or roadside trees are held to be the real murderers of all
those poor folk who crash into them at a hundred miles an
hour.

To all the causes suggested by doctors for the serious
increase in nervous disorders among students—conditions
of work, war, dope, living in big cities, abuse of tobacco,
and so on—it might be legitimate to add the perpetual
changing and switching about of the materials of instruction
and of methods of teaching, following the constant flow of
new discoveries in science and in theories of education.
"Research" has invaded our schools and universities, in a
spirit of reform and experience, always with the aim of
forming the pupil, but by a process of formation which is
always changing, so that the atmosphere of our classrooms
is gradually becoming more and more like that of a workshop.

A convinced Christian cannot help groaning with dismay,
for love of his fellow men and of the Church, the enormous
burden of whose task he clearly perceives, when he sees the
injustice and the chaos in this technological world—beginning with the accumulation of material goods by Christian
peoples; but neither can he give way to despair, since he
shares an eternal hope. Even if it involves his suffering, he
must look at the other side of technology; he must walk on
rotting timbers, if that is where men live. The light that
shines in the darkness is the same that can shed light on
men's neuroses. The twilight of certain forms of reasoning is
not necessarily the same as that of adoration. Look again at
the Bible and the whole complicated—even chaotic—story
of the expectation and the coming of the Messiah: all the
confusion, all the trials of the "diaspora" find there their

pattern. Are we driven mad by the troubles of our contemporary society, by the insecurity of the peace of the world, or of governments, or of our education? The tumultuous and blessed odyssey of the Jewish people could shed a great deal of light for us on the facts of man's present condition.

St John says, in his account of the Passion, "And Pilate wrote out a proclamation, which he put on the cross; it ran, Jesus of Nazareth, the king of the Jews. This proclamation was read by many of the Jews, since the place where Jesus was crucified was close to the city; it was written in Hebrew, Greek and Latin." Can we not see the importance of this last phrase? Bilingual and multilingual societies, the mingling of cultures, the search for truth in different vocabularies —all this goes back to the beginnings of humanity. The unrest and agitation, even some of the madness we associate with our contemporary world, are only continuations of what has gone before.

At a time when doctors can claim to have eradicated the plague, but when one cannot fall into a big city's river without the risk of contracting some other mortal illness; when the length of a man's life has been greatly increased, but when the average physique of active people is sensibly weaker; when super-athletes break record after record, but when skiers turn up their noses at the task of walking up a slope, or when a rucksack is a picturesque relic on the backs of hitch-hikers; at such a time Christianity must constantly preach, through the hierarchy and the laity, an earthly humility, without losing sight of its eternal message. The Christian has no wish to mistrust technology *a priori*— and *must* have no mistrust: he makes a good deal of use of technology himself, as we have said. Yet he can and must be allowed to protest not only against the many practical abuses committed by technology, but also against a general tendency of technology, which seems to be natural to it, to go beyond its proper limits. At first sight, this last point is difficult to reconcile with the absence of mistrust, but in fact it is not really a major obstacle. Christianity's attitude towards technology is the same as its attitude towards man, whom it cannot mistrust because he is a creature of God, but whose sinful nature it must constantly keep in mind. It is that same human nature which casts its shadow over all technology, past, present and to come.

Christianity must therefore maintain, in those minds and spirits who acknowledge the authority of its dogmas, a spirit of deep reflection and investigation concerned with the grand-sounding terms used by supporters of technology— man's advance, meaning of history, barbarism, wasted energy, and so on—which are generally very far from clear and simple. Technocrats and higher technologists may claim that they are not concerned to play with words: they do have to speak sometimes, or someone has to speak for them, and most often they speak in order to foretell or to lay down what sort of shattering future is in store for us, in cold and somewhat sibylline terms. For they know themselves to be, or are told that they are, the lords of the earth.

Christianity must take to pieces and examine views such as these. It has a ready understanding of the men of our times, of their confusions, their frenzies, their neuroses, their weaknesses, their needs and desires; and it must try to show them that it really is, in its depth, and because it is suited to all peoples and places and times, the faith for the present time. It knows the slums and the skyscraper hotels; it can talk with scientists and philosophers; it believes, within certain limits, in the benefits of sport and films and television; sermons and pastoral letters draw regularly and readily on contemporary life for their metaphors and their examples. But with this ready and willing approach to modern men, observing them and loving them, Christianity must nevertheless strictly watch that it concedes nothing to a cult or worship of the slogans of the age. The various organizations of Catholic Action take up the cause of material progress as part of their work—one thinks of the Association of Catholic Trades Unionists, who in their way take up again the work of the medieval guilds and corporations; they need not hesitate to base their arguments for technology on their religion, for it is only one of the means of their apostolate. Their essential aims are not increased production figures, nor better hours of work, but progress in Christian joy, in the Communion of the Saints.

But twentieth-century priests must not suggest that Christ believed in or supported technological progress. Anticlerics of all kinds, and even friendly humorists, have successfully debunked the idea of the alliance of the sword and the aspergillum, although, at its highest, chivalry directly depended on the great Christian virtues—the knight St Martin with a sweep of his sword sharing his cloak with a beggar: both a mark of chivalry and of Christianity; or St Francis of Assisi abandoning all his goods in an instant; or St Joan of Arc. Though we are not unaware in what intrigues was dissipated the spirit of the Crusades.

The traps are countless; how can we affirm that we shall avoid them every time? The priests in certain poor parishes, working in de-Christianized areas of factories and slums, sometimes cannot help simplifying the Gospel message and giving it a materialist meaning: they are tempted to cry, "Woe unto you, Pharisees and hypocrites!" and to develop a teaching which comes to be a sort of class struggle. Yet, as they preach a religion of love, they drown their difficulties in the longing for the coming of a true and just workers' civilization, a society of great-hearted technologists directing works of happiness.

And the Trinity, original sin, the mystery of the Church? There is a tendency to leave all this in the background: we shall come to that later. It is more important first, by showing men that one has a brother's understanding for their daily struggles, to restore to them their dignity as persons. Only, catechumens are hardly thus encouraged to take a deep personal interest in the mystical content of their faith. There is a great danger that the relationship between laity and clergy will be one of "I will show you that workers' problems are taken into account in the Church, and then you trust me as to the rest". In such a situation, the sacrifice of the Mass might become a ceremony attended as of right only, and there would be no communion with the eternal and universal prayers of the Church.

Ubi caritas et amor . . . ("Where charity and love are"). We have no right, nor would we have any desire, to judge those parish priests who might in their great love and charity so colour the Church's message. Anyone who has lived in mining country or near great industrial works or in great commercial ports knows full well how difficult it is to avoid doing so. Is it only demagogy when one smiles at a child in order to make contact, or strokes the feathers of a wounded bird? Did not Christ say that before a man makes his offering he should first be reconciled with his brother?

No doubt it would be better if . . . but this may be left to the priests themselves. So far as we are concerned, there are other more private, more numerous failures which shock us more, and those generally in better class parishes, where there is no shortage of money. Their characteristic is a kind of smug and sanctimonious optimism which is as far from true Christian joy as is the beauty of a waxen image from that of the warm and living flesh itself. The middle classes in the technological age: they go to Mass, and Christ dies again on the cross—it is a good and beautiful routine on a Sunday morning. And outside the church stand the rows of cars to take these Christians comfortably away, to protect them from the dusty roads between the church and their homes.

Am I exaggerating? Surely not. And we can forgive the

parish priests: they are subtly intoxicated by their surroundings, like teetotallers who get drunk on the smell of alcohol. There are too many things about them in the streets and houses of their parishes which speak of comfort and technical well-being, and the pleasure of talking of progress and its various forms. What is money? It is a kind of small game, very tasty and very plentiful; when you want some, you go out and *draw* a cheque—just like that, like a partridge you can't miss.

A system of thought is not to be measured by such distortions and perversions. The Church of God encourages technology only so far as it makes it easier for man to glorify God, to serve God in serving his fellow men. The Gospel is not a message of misery or beggary. A man must have bread when his children ask him for it, so that he is not forced to offer them a stone; he must have a roof over his head and a job. For a man to accept the faith with its difficulties and its splendours, which requires leisure to think and reflect, he must be rescued from the darkness of that misery which makes him an animal or a thing, a shapeless and nameless bit of a mass (*proles*). The difference between that misery and poverty is not one of degree only, but of kind, of essence; just as when a man comes out of prison the distance between his cell and freedom is not to be measured in yards. When the brutalizing and disgraceful slavery of that misery has been abolished, a man can breathe and move freely, in a poverty that stimulates the spirit.

Christianity can welcome technology when—and it is not always proved to do so—it frees men from misery for a blessed poverty; but that is the extent of its welcome: it has no call to thank the power that makes poor men rich. Nor, of course, to criticize it, as such; but the process must be watched, and this modern cornucopia so full of good things used properly. The dangers are very great, but Hope is not to be put off by them. As always, there is good reason why

Hope is joined with the Christian faith. It is not always certain that the worst will happen, and we can believe Hope when she says in a small but firm voice that nothing is lost, today or tomorrow. Let us stand by this Hope. We have recognized the great perspicacity of these Christian opponents of technology in their analysis of the situation; but even though we understand their anger and their antagonism, we cannot share it, nor agree with the rejection of technology in which it must end.

There can perhaps be righteous anger and antagonism. Christ, of course, was angry with the merchants in the Temple: but this was not anger against technologists or technocrats, but against hypocrites. Antagonism against technology cannot be righteous, and must falsify the final verdict, by prejudging the issue.

We cannot reconcile faith and technology by appealing to God the watchmaker; no more can we reject technology altogether by appealing to the anger or antagonism of God.

CHAPTER VI

THE WORLD TODAY

A Christian who fully lives his faith ought to be less bound up with this world than an agnostic, for the doctrines of that faith tell him over and over again that his earthly existence is but temporary: he has intimations of eternity. He cannot grant to the present in which he lives any right to be called more "real" than any other moment in history. But if it is therefore impossible for him to accept Hegel's ideas, he can nevertheless perceive in them some elements of truth. There are texts enough in the Scriptures which proclaim clearly that our neighbour should stand, for us, for Christ himself. Simply because he lives *sub specie aeternitatis* the Christian cannot, therefore, lack sympathy or true friendship towards the living creatures about him and their struggles. Technology has made travel so fast and exchange of information so nearly instantaneous, that the "neighbour" of the Gospel has become every man on earth.

But before we examine some of the various ways and places in which Christianity and technology live together more or less harmoniously in the world today, let us guard against a Leibnizian optimism which that examination might engender. Comfort is often taken nowadays from the fact that young people show such great interest in music and the arts; not merely superficially, but so as to be able to listen and look and criticize intelligently. And if the experts now advise us against keeping a car more than two years, it is on the other hand now recognized that the material remains of past ages must be preserved. Nor does this respect for the monuments of the past recognize any political frontiers or iron curtains: Nasser floodlights the pyramids just as the English do Winchester Cathedral or the Austrians the Hofburg. When the Poles rebuilt Warsaw, they did it with the same faithfulness to the past as did the architects of St Malo. The Kremlin in Moscow and the Imperial Palace in Peking are maintained with the same jealous care as the monuments of ancient Rome or the old buildings of Venice or the gardens of Versailles.

No doubt a great deal could be said about the profound sentiments which inspire such behaviour. But one thing must be said: this age of technology is not entitled to claim for itself the merits of works produced in the past, simply because of a craze for art, or because technology can do such wonderful things in preserving such monuments and saving them from destruction. If we sleep in old beds, eat from old china and glass, and walk in old gardens, it is not because we are better than the men of old, but for the simple reason that we come after them. And this should make us humble. Simply because we live now, we enjoy a far greater range of possibilities of knowledge than our predecessors, from whom we have received as their heirs all they had acquired, good and bad together. When we laud the advantages and merits of our technological civilization, let us be careful not to include in the picture those good things which are not truly ours.

Modern sociologists have often said that a civilization based on work, which is the state into which the world ought to move in the near future, will bring into being its daughter civilization, one of leisure. Now there is nothing in this which is theoretically opposed to the hopes of Christians. But while we can admit that technology can help to build a civilization based on work, we cannot easily see it helping, even indirectly, to build a real civilization of leisure. It can make factories to produce games and toys and tranquillizers; it cannot produce contentment or rest or pleasant strolls. We quickly tire of films and radio and television; we should be better off with art and sport and travel. But this is to say that technology cannot have it all its own way in its transformation of the world. Technology can now, in its present state, make the heritage left to us by men of the past bear great fruit: it must not be allowed to destroy it or sell it for hard cash by over-industrializing the world too quickly. When the world has been filled with factories and suburbs, it will be too late to start thinking about Leisure. Modern technology has a very loud voice: but if it trumpets forth the names of Mozart or van Gogh or the masters of Romanesque architecture, it still cannot claim the credit for these artists. When a theology of beauty is developed—and beauty is one of the essential attributes of divinity—it may establish that among the many riches offered by art for our human pleasure, very few can properly be put down to the credit of technological thought.

In so far as the common sense of the Gospels has been assimilated into their customs and institutions, the Christian nations of Europe have avoided the twin dangers of intellectual stagnation and the feverish cult of technological progress. Which is not to say that they have emerged into the full and perfect light of day. Even the most advanced are still threatened by great dangers, of which a nuclear war is only the most terrifyingly obvious. The dangers of spiritual sluggishness and a real enslavement of men inherent in the mad pursuit of material well-being must not be overlooked. But in most of these countries, for the time being at any rate, Christianity and technological thought are going ahead together.

It is perhaps right that the first place in our survey should go to a small country whose very existence, in the most physical meaning of that word, is extraordinarily significant. For long before there was talk of atom bombs, ever since her most remote origins, Holland has lived as she does now under an almost permanent threat. A great part of the soil of Holland lies below sea level, and if that area were long recaptured by the water, the rest would not be worth very much. Now the Dutch did their share of fighting in the wars of religion; but, Catholics or Protestants, they have always shown throughout the centuries, in the vital defence of their land against wind and tide, where the spirit of technology can be reconciled with Christianity. As has already been pointed out, *homo faber* was not yet *homo technicus*. But the careful ingenuity, the studious spirit of inquiry, and the willingness to organize themselves collectively so consistently manifested by generations and generations of Dutchmen in their war against the waves and the sea surely make the long prosperity of their land a sort of tremendous success for technology, more magnificent than the hanging gardens of Babylon or the Leaning Tower of Pisa or the Suez Canal. Hardly anywhere in the world, not even in Denmark, are agricultural production figures so high, though this has not prevented the rise of industry. An abundance of grey matter more than makes up for any lack of subsoil in a land that loves business, so that otherwise inevitable emigration has been checked and this small country has a greater density of population than any other country in the world, not excepting Japan.

We have stressed the case of Holland, a half-Catholic, half-Protestant country, out of all the cases of Christian countries and others where religion is a real part of life, because it seems to be fairly typical, considering the possibilities today. It is even, more or less, a success: relations between Christianity and technology must still be investigated and always improved, but in Holland a balance has already been struck.

With the exception of Spain and Portugal, which must not be condemned too hastily—they have first to overcome serious difficulties of habit or economics—the Catholic countries of Europe have unreservedly and confidently undertaken to work with technology. The most recent example—how significantly!—is that of Ireland. The isle of saints, so contemptuous of reality and its demands, has lately conceived the desire to set up her own industry. Plans have been drawn up by experts; and in this she is again in step with Rome, for now all Italy, where the process began much earlier, has made the same choice, and calls on technology to guarantee material subsistence. Catholic inspiration has helped the economy of the peninsula much more vigorously and healthily than Fascism ever could. Everyone can see that the religious convictions of a Silone or La Pira are the same as those of a Don Bosco or Padre Pio.

If some Christians are so afraid of their own time and of the future that their fear casts a shadow, for many non-Christians, over the sun, the *sol invictus*, of Christ, that fear scarcely seems to exist in West Germany, where a comparatively short space of time has been sufficient for a powerful recovery, both material and spiritual. The Nazi régime made considerable and spectacular use of technology on various levels: party organization, propaganda, the organization of workers, the persecution of the Jews, the fifth columns, the concentration camps . . . in such dirt and filth technology itself might have been stained. But technology was not on trial at Nuremberg, nor was it mentioned in the indictment. All the while the arguments went on, technology went to work in the ruins of the great cities shattered by the bombing and showed that, despite its involvement with the Nazis, it was no more a party member than the air or the rain or the light of the sun. German Catholicism, whose leaders were persecuted by Hitler, has vigorously and most usefully helped to clear technology. Always enamoured of high theology, it nevertheless kept its feet on the ground, with a feeling for organization and for what will work. And now that Germany enjoys economic prosperity, it is aware of the spiritual dangers threatening the country, but still confidently works for a world in which technology will contribute more to religion than it does today.

The United States has given a name to a material structure, a pattern of behaviour, a state of mind, against which many western European writers from Duhamel to Huxley have reacted, as well as Americans from Poe to Sinclair Lewis and Hemingway, but which remain massive and incontestable facts: the "American way of life" is an essential component of the modern world and of technological civilization. Objects, ideas and vocabulary have crossed the Atlantic as signs of a world in which series of mechanisms have finally made certain of the victory of man over matter. Man can now organize his life and enjoy its comforts.

It is an optimistic country, rich in resources and in industrial enterprise, and of growing power, so that it cannot doubt that there must be a clear solution to every problem.

Two great waves of Americanism broke over the world, after the two world wars, after 1918 and 1945. It is not by accident that the United Nations building is in New York; nor is it chance if the various criteria used by international organizations to determine the "level of civilization" (it is not yet measured in minutes or in microns, but that will come; already we are given figures, as if for the height of a tide, for the "standard of living") are shamelessly plagiarized from a behaviourist psychology now out of fashion in Europe. You tell me how many refrigerators you have and I will tell you where you stand on the ladder of civilization. Cheerfulness, kindness, sympathy, a feeling for others, a sense of wonder—all this is superfluous: we must talk about the economics of hospital services, the number of nightclubs, the attendances at museums or cinemas, the length of the railroads, the size of the newspapers, the number of cars or telephones or television sets or washing-machines.

Such a materialist way of life ought perhaps to have led to widespread public and private paganism. It has been seen too clearly in Europe how the decline of religious observance follows the establishment of factories, and the shift of workers from the country into the towns. Urban and industrial life frees the individual from his old environment and beliefs only to imprison him in monotonous, repetitive work, in the clap-trap of ideologies, and temptations to material luxuries that have become necessities; it deprives him of that minimum of time for reflection without which a man cannot live his full spiritual life. How much more should this be true of the melting-pot of the American cities, those mushroom towns built and destroyed and rebuilt by wave after wave of immigrants?

Such fears might well be felt by one who has suffered the shock to the senses produced by a modern American city: these great buildings sing so loudly of the power of matter, of visible goods, of the dollar. Nor is the mind allowed to be mistaken for a moment as to where lies the heart that directs all this bustle, this concentration of material goods: there in the sky-scrapers are the vital organs of the city, the banks, the insurance companies, the giant hotels. Technological civilization does not here aspire to rival God in his work: it is quite happy in itself, admiring itself.

But although these fears might be felt by Europeans, the United States firmly gives the lie to them. The United States is an original human community, and is not to be judged by a certain bad influence which Americans do spread a little all over the world, but which is perhaps more demanded by foreigners than forced on them. Even if "the American way of life"—which is a phrase of wider and more subtle meaning than one might think—does not necessarily denote an acceptable religious ideal, it does imply the exercise of real virtues, and provides a good many weak people with a sound basis for morality.

If the United States is a stronghold of technology, it is no citadel of irreligion. If we could trust the tone of politicians' speeches or the statistics for attendance at church or in the temples and synagogues, we might be tempted to take this country as a pattern and build great hopes for the future relations between technology and religion. But we must not be carried away. We need to consider with very great care public behaviour—"publicity" even—in a country which has gone so far in the expert exploitation of myths: the film star, the party leader, the rich philanthropist, and so on. As for "behaviourism" in general, we may consider it a false doctrine, irreconcilable with the wisdom and nobility of a Gospel which so clearly distinguishes between the letter and the spirit.

But where the letter reflects the spirit we must not condemn it. Without going into raptures over the obvious development of American religious life, we must surely admire the genuine health of the Catholic Church in the United States. The election of John F. Kennedy as President was significant; and even more significant was his first presidential address to Congress, impregnated with a calm and reasoned faith in the future of man and of the world, a faith which has its source in Christianity, and finds its greatest earthly encouragement in technology. The Catholic Church in the United States is strong and vigorous, and growing: in the ten years from 1952 to 1962, it increased its numbers by two-fifths to nearly forty-three million, one of the highest figures in the world, with a numerous secular and regular clergy and flourishing houses of the contemplative orders.

The picture has its darker elements, as always when we are dealing with the souls of men, but even if we must say so, we must not forget the light: the balance sheet is in credit. We can say that in the United States Catholicism has taken a position with regard to technology and techniques which is full of confidence and friendship and which on the one hand respects the nature of technology and on the other ensures that the common people know it better and look on it with a friendly eye.

On the darker side, we may mention the extraordinary percentage of Americans who put "No religion" in the appropriate column in official census returns. This betrays an odd flaw in the national system. The American way of life claims to require attachment to a religion and obedience to its rules; an atheist is surely an asocial being. The references to the divinity which are made so often in official pronouncements and speeches really embroider the reality, it seems, and testify to a conformism to an order which is somewhat of an illusion.

The strength of the American democracy, we are told, rests on the civic feelings and the common will of its members working together. How is it, then, that in the presidential elections—which ought to have been a great occasion for essential participation in the life of the nation—half of those entitled to vote did not bother? There are many causes for this regularly recurring phenomenon, but a good deal of the responsibility must rest on technology's shoulders. Too many individual Americans, spoiled and unbalanced and even made too machine-like by the noise and routine of their daily work, left the choice to their fellow-citizens.

On November 16th, 1961, the American bishops issued a statement after their annual conference which significantly sounded the alarm. The serious and even solemn prose and the calm and genuine hope in the peroration cannot conceal the unusually strong feelings in the preceding denunciations:

Everywhere can be seen evidence of the moral decline of our nation: in the alarming growth in the number of crimes, particularly among the young; in the sensational exploitation of violence in the press and in films, on the stage and television screen; in the discovery of shameless corruption in the government and in business; and in survivals of race hatred and injustice.

Our present moral deterioration cannot be regarded as a passing weakness which will be followed by such a moral amendment as past experience might make us hope for. The conditions we meet today are unique, and in such conditions the past can offer us neither precedent nor guidance. Many men now deny any objective distinction between good and evil, or any ability of man's reason to know certainly what is good and what evil; such men separate themselves from all past traditions of morality.

Not only do many Americans now live as if there were no God to whom they must give account, but a growing number —among whom are some who wield great power—declare that the non-existence of God is a scientifically established fact.

It is a severe judgement: "moral decline" is taken to be a fact beyond discussion, and it is described as no "passing weakness".

The bishops look for the remedy. Without putting Catholicism in a position of withdrawal (as a minority, they could have blamed other Churches) they called men back to a respect for principles. We cannot quote it all, but one sentence is most significant: "Above all the climate of our times demands that we all personally bear witness by our words and our actions to the existence of moral principles based on our religious beliefs." The bishops wanted to publish a comparatively short statement. In the absence of an analysis which would have brought them to naming technology, they show in the very formulation of their demand that they recognize the breakdown of American man for which technology is guilty: "The climate of our times demands that we all *personally* bear witness. . . ." The accent is on the irreplaceable value of the human person, that poor human person of whom adversaries of technology such as Marcel and Bernanos claim to be the best defenders. It is now beyond any doubt a matter of reacting and fighting against the "robotization" of man produced, slowly and surely, by mechanization, by material comforts, by the pressures of social life.

It may now be asked, "If it is now grappling with a moral decline of which you do not think technology innocent, how can the most "technologized" nation in the world have anything positive to offer to the argument?" I do not wish to avoid this fair objection, any more than I would retract my optimism with regard to the American experience. I accept the fact of moral decline; the American bishops would not have exercised their spiritual authority over a triviality. They must have been reluctant, at a time and in a world in which political ideologies shamelessly exploit such news, to seem to be providing such capital to the many enemies of their country. Since they speak of it, we can take it that the United States is in the throes of a moral crisis which is unparalleled, and we have the right to hold the abuses of technology gravely responsible.

We can go further. This moral decline is surely not peculiar to the American democracy; it is possible, even likely, that almost every country, especially those in which technological advance is swiftest, is being similarly affected. It is a decline, as the American bishops say, which will go on, and "the past can offer us neither precedent nor guidance". Because of technology, the world is experiencing a time when the help promised by Christ is still there for men, but when men themselves, disorientated and lost, no longer know whether they want it. We are perhaps in a period when material advance and moral decline go together. Atheism temporarily satisfies plain and simple souls scandalized by the unchristian behaviour of many Christians, as well as those who prefer a swift and apparently liberating solution, like cutting the Gordian knot, to a difficult personal search for truth.

In Russia, atheism is official, and the fight against religion is waged strongly in a country which theoretically recognizes the freedom of the individual's conscience. Contrary to what many people think, technology was not introduced into Russia by Marxist Leninism. Even before the 1914–18 war, Russian science could boast some great names, and industrialization, largely with the aid of foreign capital, had begun. But it remains true, of course, that a gigantic effort has been made by the Soviet régime to speed up the process. It has always been part of official doctrine, and Lenin's definition is well known: "Communism is the power of the soviets plus the electrification of the whole country." And we can remember with what violence the old rural economy was broken down between the wars, while great shipyards, such as those at Dnieprostroi, and enormous factories were built. The free world, which was still discussing the merits of a planned economy, was stupefied by Russia's first Five Year Plan, though the lesson was not lost on Dr Schacht or Roosevelt's advisers. Meanwhile, technology ruled internal politics, with its single party disciplined like a machine, and its mass instruments, *agitprop*, and so on.

On the red ground of the national flag are a crossed hammer and sickle. By joining thus the symbols of the two essential categories of the population, the government showed that the country was no longer in the stage of small family businesses with divergent interests, but that the Russian people now formed a unique whole, a vast unity of workers. And if in this theoretical idea of the "worker" neither the industrial worker nor the agricultural labourer was supposed to be more important than the other, in fact the former generally triumphed over the latter, and agriculture, in being socialized, had to be mechanized and planned like any industry: it had to become technological.

With the German invasion of Russia came the revelation to the world not only of Russian patriotism but of the high standard of Russian technology. Fifteen years later that revelation became a dazzling vision as the first sputnik circled the globe. We have already seen how the Russian government uses and interprets the successes of technology as confirmation of Marxist-Leninist atheism. Russia is surely a country in which technology and religion are stated to be incompatible. Communism, by putting the riches of the world at the disposal of all, and by ceaselessly calling upon an ever more powerful technology to make production and distribution easier, has freed man from the childish myths and consolations of religion. "Prometheus can no longer be bound," says Professor Bykowsky, meaning that no Transcendence can now claim any sacred right over the energies of the cosmos, which are now all accessible to man's intelligence.

But is Russia a country of atheist technological materialism? To say so would really be cheating. Russia, like America, is an ambiguous case when considered from our point of view in this book. Technological materialism may be official, but it shows curious failings. The Christian is bound to notice the no doubt unintentional failures in agricultural development: can an over-confident technology be incapable of satisfying the basic needs of man? Sending rockets into space is very fine, but would it not be better to concentrate on men's daily bread? There is an almost puritanical voluntary restriction of the production of consumer goods, and while techniques of space travel are developing fast, much less progress is made in matters of material comfort.

There is here a strange inconsistency. Public morality profits by it, we must admit, but it is at the expense of official panegyrics on the triumph of man over matter. Behaviour is essentially ruled by a sort of Spartan conformism. The family unit has become a civic thing, with nothing sacred about it, though law and custom protect it carefully. Literature and the cinema have to banish any kind of bawdiness, though they are careful not to attack it. In schools, universities and workshops, the young people are taught the "love of and respect for work", and are very serious in their pursuit of physical and artistic education. So far as things are not complicated by political propaganda, all this provides a healthy moral climate, and it is not surprising that many Christians who visit the U.S.S.R. have been led to indulge in bitter reflections on the wastefulness and triviality rampant in the United States and other western nations.

This is true: but it must be said that the credit does not belong to the historico-technological materialism of Marx and Lenin. The national virtues of the Russian people have played a much greater part than any text.

Do those virtues go back to Christian days? To some extent, perhaps. We cannot regard the U.S.S.R., a human society and not a politico-social régime, as a pagan or atheist nation. God is not dead in Russia. There is a good deal of evidence that religion enjoys a vigorous underground life: according to a reliable authority seventy-five to eighty per cent of Russian children are baptized. The Academician Mitin, president of the Society for the Development of Political and Scientific Knowledge, reported in 1957 that there had been "a partial renaissance of religion, because of a relaxing of our efforts". We may accept the first part of this phrase more readily than the second, but it is an objective judgement and very informative. Historical materialism, a theory constantly reaffirmed by the government, on which the whole development of its technology is based, has not passed into the behaviour of the people. Those who preserve or rediscover Christianity, though they must admit that they are bound to be somewhat careful and secretive about their practice of the faith, cannot see whether it is really opposed to a philosophy which is not really reflected in daily life. So an odd sort of co-existence is brought about, and it is difficult to see what the future holds, or what the exact rôle of technology will be in this respect.

There are many parts of the world we must pass over without consideration: South America, Africa, with its new nations, where Catholicism is a strong spiritual force, and one vigorously in favour of technological development, and China, where Catholics, a very small minority, are persecuted more from a sort of xenophobia than for truly doctrinal reasons, and where they certainly would not want to criticize technological advance as such. Our object has been to show that Christianity in the twentieth century almost universally encourages and supports technology. This does not mean that we should not be on our guard, to criticize and check excesses and aberrations, and to bring to people's notice any decline in morality. The world in which we live is like a vast shipyard at night, in which the arc lamps leave a thousand corners in darkness. And we await the dawn.

CHAPTER VII

MAN AND THE MEANING

OF HISTORY

Now we must come back to man, for he is what this is all about. We have been talking about countries and peoples and governments and their vast plans; we have caught a glimpse of a savage world struggling and working to extricate itself from stagnation and disorder, and we have heard its feverish appeal to every kind of technology. From this too rapid survey, with its often contradictory details, we derive the general assurance that Christianity has been true to itself in supporting the efforts of the world, but also that a truly Christian technological civilization, though there are signs of its coming discernible here and there, is still a thing to hope for in the future. Production records as such have no interest for Christianity: it must first be certain that they are not the result of some sterile pride. The only actions that matter are those that serve the human person, man.

We cannot see the divine plan working through the Communion of the Saints, but we do know for certain that it does not require the sanction of technology. It does not incline to an *ad hoc* conformity or to compromise, but jealously preserves the integrity of its field of operation, all those various good souls whom it must help assist one another until the last dawn of the *parousia*.

A few years before the war, an American film humorously satirized the piling up of material goods: it was called, "You Can't Take It with You", and no one could be in greater agreement with this sentiment than the Christian. Do not think about wealth and goods, which must be left behind: think rather of those men and women who in some way, by a look or a word or a gesture, have made you feel the truth of the words, "the greatness of the human person". There is true wealth. "Personality" has been debased in modern use, but its true meaning is untarnished: God is still worshipped in Three Persons.

Can it be said that technological civilization will ever, from its own resources, help to produce those generous and great-hearted men and women, such as we have all met, who energetically defend the cause of this modern world while their interior life is nourished from elsewhere? We can think of Péguy, Simone Weil, Raïssa Maritain, Yves Congar, Teilhard de Chardin and many others, who can accept and fit into the present world and its technology because they know how to go beyond it.

No Frenchman can now write of the sea without quoting Baudelaire; no one can write of the relations between technology and religion without reference to Bergson. He did not attack technology: it was merely not enough in itself, but needed mystery to complete it, and the world it claimed to make and organize needed spirit for its completion.

We cannot undertake a long discussion or evaluation of Bergson's ideas, but Christians can go with him freely and boldly without being cautious in their attitude. They are concerned with technological civilization, the common good of all men, and it is that civilization as a whole they are prepared to help, provided it understands the nature of their help. Plato had inscribed over the door of his school "Let no one ignorant of mathematics enter here." Modesty and the fear of hurting sincere minds prevent the Christian putting up over the entrance to the Palace of the Future, "Let no one who is not a mystic enter here", but he should work and pray to see that the spirit does indeed complete the world that is shaping itself now.

It can be seen from much that we have said, however unsystematically, about the world today, that the spiritual has been gravely weakened almost everywhere by the advance of technology. We shall now see with what great honour technology is more and more treated as the consoler of the poor, and the marvellous task which certain materially endowed Christian nations have inherited, as it were, of giving fraternal aid to peoples who are technologically underdeveloped. The world's affairs seem to move so much of their own accord that we can content ourselves with a few pages only; yet even here there are snags.

Can the materially rich Christian nations justify their own excess of material comfort by the charity they can give to poorer countries, thanks to their technology? Are they so secure in the superiority of their technical intelligence, thanks to which they have overcome their own natural scourges? Where is the greatness of a system which profits only part of the whole, gorging some by starving others? Surely it is a poor sort of technology that must conform to the shifting morality of the powerful of this world and help only the rich, while its true task is to help the weak, and, by material means, which are not to be ignored so long as the spirit breathes on them, assist the Communion of the Saints.

Without being quixotic about it, we can say that there is much more in technology than is suggested by the part it has so far been described as playing, which is, if not a caricature of its resources, at least an utterly insufficient use of them. Technology must become aware of this and be reformed. This is the business of man, and he must begin by realizing that there is much more in himself. The world is crying out for technologists and experts: along with the knowledge of their profession, each must also possess a good measure of the spirit of holiness.

The mind and body are so overwhelmed and intoxicated by noise and speed and the violence of events that a bulldozer razing buildings to the ground attracts the attention of passers-by much more readily than the silent growth of the tree whose roots also push through his concrete. But technology includes far more than mere machines, which are only its visible workshop: it has a much vaster realm—vaster and, if man wills, far nobler.

It can hardly be chance that the question of birth control has become so urgent at just the time when technology can boast of conquering all material difficulties. And is it not an absurd paradox? Man the master of nature as the victim of his own victory? The ever faster advance of technology and the unbridled march of progress are solemn principles, and the increase in the birth-rate is a calamity. Let us have more cars, more pipe-lines, more electric cables, more big buildings, more air-cushions, can-openers and cylinders of gas, but fewer men. What would happen if the advance of technology were controlled rather than the birth-rate? We must go back to Bergson: technology needs mysticism. . . . Christianity must take its part in technological civilization, and that civilization must understand and accept the necessity for Christianity's intervention.

And we may wonder, quite seriously, whether by the complement of the spirit Bergson meant, to a great extent, humour. His book, *Le Rire*, suggests that laughter is a defence of human freedom against mechanization and automatism and so on, against all the disorders psychologists constantly blame on to technology. The healthy jokes of Chaplin or Clair or Tati on the ridiculous excesses of mechanization are a sort of mystical revenge: the angel awakens in the spectator, and it is he who laughs aloud at these "Modern Times".

One of the more serious modern ideas which allies of technology love to wave about is that of the "meaning of history": according to Marx and thinkers like him, mankind and man's economy march in a particular direction, with a certainty like that of gravitation. If anti-Marxist Christians laugh at this idea, they should remember that Christian philosophy also believed that history had a meaning and direction.

But experience has forced Marxism to modify its certitudes: the end of the march of history is beyond question, the establishment of international communism; but how quickly and how it is to be achieved—these are thorny questions indeed! The inevitable shilly-shallying of Marxism in adapting its creed to events has been a matter of great interest for western technologists and experts, who have not forgotten the great depression between the wars, and who have been shaken as it were by a cold shower by the tangible progress communism has made in the world. Cannot technology, as respected in the U.S.A. as in the U.S.S.R., offer the true solution to the problem? Cannot it make it possible for capitalism to slough off its old skin and learn to coexist with communism? Technology may give its own meaning to history: twentieth-century man may be marching directly towards a marvellous domination of matter and the energy of the universe.

In itself, such an idea need neither frighten nor seduce the Christian. He too believes that history has a meaning, a direction. And technology has its proper part to play in that history, in helping to make a better world for better men.

But he must not go too fast. He can put his hope in technology, but he must not expect too much. The failures in the response of technology to the doubts and anxieties of the mind must be made up by Christianity, and Christianity must base on God the task man has been charged with carrying out in this world: "Your duty in organizing the world is not to build a final terrestrial society," Pius XII told the technologists in 1958, "but to make easier, here on earth, for yourselves and your contemporaries, the only search and the only discovery which really matter, those of God." The meaning of history does not belong to technology. It works to make that meaning clearer, and we may believe that it will make it ever more clear: but salvation does not come from technology, which must always remain a temporary and terrestrial secondary cause.

CHAPTER VIII

CHARITY AND

COMMUNITY

This is how, with a crafty show of violence, Khrushchev exalts the moral principles of "communist education" at the expense of bourgeois values:

> For more than a century bourgeois ideologists have accused communists of denying all morality. The bourgeoisie have needed this lie to conceal their own immorality. What are the bases of the moral principles of the exploiting classes? They are clearly expressed in such sayings as, "The rich and powerful can do as they please"; "You rob others, or they will rob you"; "Money has no smell"; "Man is a wolf to other men". We effectively repudiate these barbarous and cynical rules. To them we oppose the moral principles of collectivism and humanity, expressed in these beautiful phrases: "All for one, and one for all" and "Every man is to all others a friend, a comrade, a brother."

Khrushchev has perhaps forgotten a few uncomfortable facts: that the text, "Love one another", had a great influence on the fine phrases which he uses to sum up the spirit of communism, and that Marx never repudiated all his Judaeo-Christian heritage, for example. Do the terms of Russian insults for their opponents suggest that man is anything but animal to others: "rat", "snake", and so on?

And did Stalin really believe in that "One for all"? Practice must accord with preaching. The earliest Christians, at least, drew from their enemies the observation, "See how they love one another". This could scarcely be said of the "friends, comrades and brothers" of the Central Committee of the U.S.S.R.

Not to be entirely negative, the Christian may see the statement of Khrushchev as an ambitious and premature attempt to give technology an ideal. Technology is aware of its power, and wishes to play a commensurate moral rôle; but it wishes to do so alone, without appealing to any mystery: it refuses to pronounce the name of charity.

Christianity must forgive these injuries. Technology can help charity greatly, but it must be shown how, since alone it will go on falling into the sin of pride. It is good for it to be aware of its power, provided it renounces once for all its claim to act as a first cause. The Christian may believe in the possibilities of technology, but he must believe in them in a Christian way. His charity towards men must be accompanied by a love for the whole universe created by God. He must expect technology to help examine and explore and know that universe, and to exploit its resources in a wise and brotherly way guided by Christian charity. Because he loves God and his brother men and the reflection of God in the world, he can have confidence, and no power-drunk destructiveness can warp his attitude, so deeply and firmly based.

Charity's needs are immense and they increase every day. If the aid contributed by technology is still insufficient, we must recognize how great and how welcome it is. That same technology whose cynicism and violence we have noticed can show itself extraordinarily ingenious in increasing the effectiveness of its service, in attacking sickness and famine and poverty. That the needs are there we can see from a glance at the publications of the U.N.O. or U.N.E.S.C.O.,

or the reports of Christian missions, or books about India
or China, or the appeals in the advertisement columns of
our daily papers, each one a mere drop in the ocean of the
world's misery.

Civil organizations and societies in the western nations
have taken on the greater part of the charitable activities
once carried out by the regular Orders. Yet they have not
thus destroyed the meaning of charity, or, if they think they
have, they are mistaken. More than ever, in all these tasks
of aid and assistance, technology needs the mystery of
belief in an invisible "something more", of self-sacrifice
and kindness. And in the international struggle against
sickness and hunger, these qualities are even more obviously
needed. The world is looking for technologists who join
technical competence with a spirit of holiness: the ability to
draw up and quote statistics, to organize appeals and money
collections, to obtain medicines and supplies of food—all
this is an indispensable basis, but to achieve real unity
between giver and receiver more subtle means are needed
urgently. The method of giving is more important than what
is given.

If ever that was true, it is true today in this field. The
world's press make possible those "chains of kindness"
which are internationally organized, clearly spontaneously,
to speed up as much as possible from one point on the globe
to any other the spread of news or the transportation of a
sick man or a rare drug. How much better it is to report this
kind of thing than crimes! In this way the word "kindness"
enters into the language like leaven into the dough. Yet
religion and technology together could do much more. The
press reports these "chains of kindness" because it pays to;
people like to read of them, because they enjoy a race or
because it encourages the myth of the superiority of our
times. Well done, indeed; but Christianity, in the exercise
of charity through technology, has other and harder tests to

undergo, which are less obvious and less dramatic, in the lonely and rough places of the world where patience and endurance are called for rather than speed or strength. Modern technology can be a great help in the development of this sort of anonymous holiness among the laity, for those who go out as experts to isolated parts of the world, or those who take part in such schemes as Voluntary Service Overseas, are missionaries, or can be, though they have neither the name nor the habit.

If there are any who fear that this sort of technological "missionary" spirit will take the place of Christian ascesis, they can be reassured. When Christianity uses technology in the fight against disease and poverty, it is not merely being sociable in order to keep up with the times, but is strictly following its proper task. Hindus have sometimes deplored the fact that their religion has not given rise to charitable works analogous to those in Europe, or to religious institutions devoted to the care of the sick or the relief of all kinds of want. The Ramakrishna Mission, which would be the nearest thing within Hinduism to what is wanted, does not in fact deny the Christian influences which were the origin of its social work.

Because we fight against sickness and poverty, we do not have to give up preaching resignation to the inevitable. For a very long time, many churchmen have stressed this resignation. Now that technology has pushed back—in appearance, perhaps, more than in fact—the limits of what is inevitable in the field of some physical sufferings, it is absolutely right that Christian education should take this into account. But we have certainly not yet arrived at the point, nor shall we in the near future, when suffering, even purely physical suffering, will be a thing of the past. If, in an excess of gloomy romanticism, too many men wallowed in such verses as these:

An apprentice is man, and grief is his master;
He knows not himself who has felt no disaster,

there is no need to examine the world of technology too closely to see that it often goes too far in caricaturing such an attitude: man today is no longer an apprentice, but grown up, qualified; and grief no longer teaches but is in retreat, for it only serves to create complexes.

It is for Christianity to shed some light on this chaos, and re-establish a difficult balance of order, using psychoanalysis and pediatrics and so on when necessary. Technology should not throw the word "suffering" into the waste-paper basket. Poor technology, capable of so much that is good and noble, yet so easily self-blinded, self-contradictory, self-prostituted. Women are told they must suffer to be beautiful, and practise abstinence and fasting in order to avoid a "spare tyre", not for the sake of God. And men are little better off: fasting and abstinence are medieval follies and such gratuitous activities are laughable; yet as their symbol of leisure they have created an appallingly noisy machine, the juke-box, the chief characteristic of which is its absolute uselessness: the only thing it offers is the ability to keep the din going. But in spite of all this, history moves on towards the light. Religion can also use the resources of technology to clear the weeds away from man's nature. The road is long, and the patience needed longer.

Here also technology has need of mystery; and mystery can flow in through the channels of humour. Soldiers are made out of civilians, and perfection is approached through what is imperfect. We may protest at the phrase, "Suffer to be beautiful", but it uses the word "suffer", and refers to the exercise of a discipline. The word can be freed again and restored to its tragic meaning, and we can pass from this to the idea of a weekly family fast to help the "war on want".

Some men and women imagined that the columns of the Temple were broken when Pius XII declared officially that there was nothing wrong with painless childbirth, especially since the methods he referred to were discovered by Soviet doctors, and they quoted Genesis against the pope. But technology was not destroying an article of faith, but only simplifying a problem of practical morality. Mothers love their children no less because they suffer much less in childbirth; and no exercises or anaesthetics can alter the fact that a mother's love is one of the great schools of pain.

Now we are coming to the end of this little book, in which an attempt has been made to describe unflinchingly the abuses and injustices of technology, it may be possible to assert more strongly the hope that this modern world, thanks to the gifts of technology and in spite of its excesses, is becoming more catholic, in becoming daily more universalized, more united, with its innumerable individual unities of men's minds increasingly in accord with one another, with "the other man", with that unknown and distant brother, the Incarnation of Christ.

When we point out to keen advocates of technological advance the excesses for which technology may be blamed, they are shocked, and want us to give technology time to put things right. But they are the very people who believe that technology must advance more rapidly, that material changes must happen more and more swiftly and ruthlessly. This is all wrong: either the advance of technology must be halted some time, or its abuses and excesses, far from being cured, will be intensified and multiplied.

But technology is not only a matter of long-term hypotheses; it is a matter of contemporary realities. The refusal to give technology *carte blanche* for an unfathomable future does not imply a desire to ignore it in our own times, when there are so many tasks it can undertake for the good of men. Valéry restricted himself to saying that we "must

try to live ": the Christian, who has received the Revelation
of God, knows that we must live, we must love life and hand
it on. Before we work for the year 2100, we must work for
the year 2000, or for 1980: and that involves difficulties
enough. The Christian must accept with joy the task of
helping the creation of a technological civilization, first and
foremost because Christianity is a joyful religion, and also
because that technological civilization will help, if only a
very little, towards the creation of man's happiness in the
future.

We believe firmly in the Christian meaning of history.
But Pius XII taught us that that belief does not imply, *ipso
facto*, belief in a long, straight-line development:

> The worshipper of the new-born Son of God knows that
> original sin and its consequences have deprived man, not of
> his domination over the earth, but of security in the exercise
> of that domination; and he also knows that, despite the fall
> consequent upon that first sin, man is still able, according to
> his destiny, to make history, but that he can only advance with
> difficulty, through a tangle of hopes and fears, of riches and
> poverty, of heights and depths, life and death, security and
> incertitude, until the last decision at the gates of eternity.

The possibilities for technology in the realm of charity
are becoming daily clearer. Through technology men can,
in their individual lives and in their life together as a whole,
show how much they love one another, in their ideas and
behaviour, and through material gifts and organizations.
Christians facing the sufferings and miseries of the modern
world see their task as a great and urgent one; but they take
it up, and the help of technology to speed up their action
and make it more effective should never pose more than
problems of detail. In the service of Christian charity,
technology is another weapon in the armoury of the spirit.
The geographical conditions of catholicity are now assured:
messengers have now gone out to the ends of the earth, and

prayers are offered by every people. Whatever we may say about the divisions of the modern world, its present constitution in three blocs is far closer to the ideal unity of this earth in God than was the Holy Roman Empire: Cardinal Feltin has pointed out that at the last General Council in 1870 some Christian nations did not send their own delegates—not only was Africa unrepresented, but the United States was represented by a European country—whereas in 1962 the assembled Fathers at the Council were far more representative of the nations of the world.

There is hope, then, for individual men and for the collectivity in which they are all united, in the friendly and close cooperation between Christianity and technology.

SELECT BIBLIOGRAPHY

In this series: ABELÉ, Jean, S.J.: *Christianity and Science*; CHAUCHARD, Paul: *Science and Religion*; LE TROCQUER, René: *What is Man?*; MORAY, N., *Cybernetics*.

BALTHASAR, H. U. von: *Science, Religion and Christianity*, translated by Hilda Graef, London, Burns and Oates, and Westminster, Md, The Newman Press, 1958.

BERGSON, H.: *Creative Evolution*, translated by A. Mitchell, London, Macmillan, 1911, and New York, Modern Library, 1944; *Laughter*, translated by C. Brereton and F. Rothwell, London, Macmillan, 1921, and New York, Doubleday, 1956.

BIVORT DE LA SAUDÉE, J. (Editor): *God, Man and the Universe*, London, Burns and Oates, and New York, Kenedy, 1954.

DUBARLE, D., O.P.: *Scientific Humanism and Christian Thought*, translated by Reginald F. Trevett, London, Blackfriars, 1956.

MARCEL, G.: *Men against Humanity*, translated by G. S. Fraser, London, Harvill Press, and Chicago, Regnery, 1952.

MARITAIN, J.: *Redeeming the Time*, London, Sheed and Ward, and New York, Hillary, 1943; *Science and Wisdom*, London, Bles, and New York, Scribner, 1944.

MASCALL, E. L.: *Christian Theology and Natural Science*, London, Longmans, 1956, and New York, Ronald Press, 1957.

RAVEN, C. E.: *Natural Religion and Christian Theology*, two volumes, Cambridge and New York, Cambridge Univ. Press, 1953.

TAYLOR, F. Sherwood: *Two Ways of Life*, London, Burns and Oates, 1947; *Man and Matter*, London, Chapman and Hall, 1951.

WHITE, Victor, O.P.: *God and the Unconscious*, London, Collins, and New York, Harper, 1952; *Soul and Psyche*, London, Collins, and New York, Harper, 1960.